Out of the Depths

A Survivor's Story of the Sinking of the USS *Indianapolis*

As Told By
Edgar Harrell, USMC

Written By
David Harrell

PRESS

Dedicated to my shipmates,
the crew of the USS *Indianapolis*.

Life is filled with gale force winds that cause the waves to roar;
And like the men of Galilee we strain against the oar.

With billows high we cry aloud, "Oh Lord, where have you gone?"
Then He whispers through the squall, "I've been here all along."

Oh we of little faith, why doubt? Why give our hearts to fear?
For when the tempest trials blow, 'tis then we must draw near!

For in the wind of every storm a Sovereign eye doth see,
The waning faith and broken hearts of those like you and me.

And with His outstretched hand of love, He reaches down to save,
All who trust in Him alone; for us His life He gave!

So when the tumults o'er us roll, let's thank Him for the gale,
For in His love He caused the storm, 'twas He who set the sail.

By David Harrell; derived from an exposition of Matthew 14:22-33.

CONTENTS

⚓

FOREWORD

By Oliver L. North, LtCol USMC, (Ret.)

"Have courage! It is I. Do not be afraid."

Mt 14:27

When that command was issued more than twenty centuries ago, it was to a group of fearful men, in peril on a dark and dangerous sea. No exhortation is more appropriate to this chronicle than those words of Jesus Christ.

On the night of 30 July 1945, just weeks before the end of World War II, the Japanese submarine *I-58* launched a spread of torpedoes at the USS *Indianapolis*. Two of the "fish" found their mark. In less than 15 minutes the heavy cruiser, a battle-scarred veteran of the bloody campaigns for the Marianas, Iwo Jima and Okinawa went down without a trace—and without anyone but the survivors knowing the ship had been lost.

Some 900 of the ship's 1,196-man crew—cold, oil-soaked, many with injuries—were suddenly alone in the shark infested waters of the Philippine Sea. For five horrific days after the sinking their numbers were cruelly depleted by shark attacks, salt-water poisoning, hypothermia and dehydration. When they were finally spotted and rescued, only 317 remained alive. This is their story, recounted by one of their own—Edgar Harrell—a young member of the U.S. Marine Ship's Detachment. It is an unparalleled account of perseverance, courage, self-sacrifice and faith.

*   *   *   *

It has been my great blessing to spend most of my life in the company of heroes. By "hero" I mean a person who has wittingly put himself in grave physical jeopardy for the benefit of another. Heroes are people who overcome evil by doing good at great personal risk. Through self-sacrifice, fortitude and action—whether they succeed or fail—heroes provide a moral and ethical frame-work—and inspiration—for the rest of us.

Unfortunately our modern definition of "hero" has been stretched to include all manner of people who do not warrant the title. The athlete who just set a new sports record isn't a hero. Nor is the "daring" movie star or even the adventurer out to be the first solo climber to scale Mt. Everest. They may be brave—but they

don't meet the definition of a hero for whatever they achieve bene-
fits only "self."

Real heroes are selfless. My father was one. Many of the
Marines with whom I was privileged to serve for nearly a quarter of
a century were heroes. The firemen and police who rushed into the
World Trade Center buildings and the Pentagon on 9-11 fit the
description. Today, a good number of the young soldiers, sailors,
airmen, Marines and Guardsmen that I cover in Iraq and
Afghanistan for FOX News certainly meet the criteria. And Edgar
Harrell, survivor of the catastrophic sinking of the USS
Indianapolis, is a hero.

*   *   *   *

The true story Edgar Harrell and his son David recount in the
pages that follow is far more than a tale of terror on the sea.
Together, they have prepared a timely and relevant work—not just
for the anniversary of a catastrophe—but for a new generation of
Americans once again confronting an enemy that teaches young
men not how to live—but how to die the right way. The kamikaze
pilot who crashed his plane into the *Indianapolis* on March 31,
1945 differs little from the nineteen terrorists of 9-11 or the suicide
car-bomber trying to kill U.S. soldiers and Marines today in Iraq.
The brutal atrocities perpetrated in the "slaughter houses" of
Fallujah are surreally similar to those committed by the Japanese

against American prisoners of war—even to posing for cameras in the midst of the evil deed.

All of that—and much more—is in this book. It is a gripping tale of men tested beyond anything they thought possible—and how they responded with bravery, endurance and faith in the face of fear and overwhelming despair. Edgar Harrell is not the only hero in this book. But his faith is a testament to the Marine Corps motto: *Semper Fidelis*—Latin for "Always Faithful."

Oliver L. North, LtCol USMC (Ret.)
Host of "War Stories"
FOX News Channel

Where can I go from Thy Spirit?

Or where can I flee from Thy presence?

If I ascend to heaven, Thou art there;

If I make my bed in Sheol, behold, Thou art there.

If I take the wings of the dawn,

If I dwell in the remotest part of the sea,

Even there Thy hand will lead me,

And Thy right hand will lay hold of me.

Psalm 139:7-10

INTRODUCTION

⚓

It is easy to grow up in the United States of America and take for granted the wonderful freedom we enjoy. I confess that I have been guilty of being unintentionally indifferent about our nation's liberty and perhaps even harboring an unwitting apathy concerning the wars that bought it. All too often Memorial Day and Veterans' Day come and go with little serious reflection about the enormous sacrifices that have been made. Maybe this describes you as well. However, the bubble of peace and prosperity that once preserved my cavalier attitude was suddenly popped by the terrorist attack of 9/11. Instantly, all Americans saw with their own eyes what evil looks like, up close and personal. Immediately our false sense of security exploded along with the Twin Towers, the Pentagon and United Flight 93 in a Pennsylvania field. With shocking abruptness, we were all reminded that freedom is not free—a simple yet profound truth our veterans know all too well.

Because of 9/11, I began to think deeply about our nation's history. Like never before the stark realities of past wars and the valiant men and women who fought them were thrust into the forefront of my mind. Almost overnight I developed a keen awareness of the unspeakable evil that plunged us into World War II—the same kind of wickedness that now plagues the world through radical Islam. I also began thinking about the part my father played in that war, along with his shipmates aboard the USS *Indianapolis*.

I remember Dad's reaction to 9/11 was simply, "Here we go again." He was right. The same diabolical evil that motivated our enemies in World War II was once again at work. And once again, men and women of valor must take up arms to ward off barbaric aggressors; heroic soldiers willing to give their lives to preserve our freedom. But what is sad is how quickly we forget the noble military contributions of the past.

I remember hearing Dad talk about the war from time to time when I was a little boy. I recall his reluctant stories about the secret mission of the *Indianapolis*, the atomic bomb components they carried, and especially the gripping tales about the sharks when the crew was lost at sea for five days. I even remember attending some of the *Indianapolis* reunions and meeting Captain McVay and being awestruck by his white Navy uniform and medals. But the depth and breadth of my father's sacrifice, and that of all the other World War II veterans, did not really grip my heart until 9/11. That mind-boggling catastrophe was a life-altering event for me, and for many

Americans. Personally, I became a man on a mission. Not just to tell my father's story and honor the crew of the USS *Indianapolis*, but to raise the awareness of the cost of freedom and the need to aggressively take up arms to defend our country. I also wanted to rekindle the fires of true, God-honoring patriotism and respect for our veterans in an apathetic, and unfortunately, historically ignorant America. Fortunately, Dad agreed with my goals, but with even greater passion due to his personal experience.

My father, like many other World War II veterans, has had many opportunities to speak around the country in a variety of venues, including public schools. In interviewing him to write this book, I was saddened to hear him tell about the prevailing ignorance most students have concerning World War II. He indicated that even many of the teachers and administrators he has met admitted they knew very little about the war, not to mention the USS *Indianapolis* tragedy. Many agreed that they were victims of a politically correct culture bent on revising history textbooks, hoping to erase the collective memory of the weapons of mass destruction used at Hiroshima and Nagasaki. This only fueled my fire to collaborate with my ex-Marine father in defending the use of the atomic bombs, not to mention educating readers about the heroism of our veterans and ultimately glorifying God who divinely superintended the freedom and prosperity we currently enjoy as Americans.

Moreover, as I interviewed Dad and other veterans about patriotism past and present, I quickly noticed how upset they would get with contemporary anti-war activists. I wholeheartedly share their frustration. I am profoundly offended by the very vocal and misguided peace activists that constantly malign our government's commitment to protect its citizens. Although I realize many are merely driven by anti-American sentiment and a naïve anthropology that has no concept of the depth of human depravity, there are others who wish to argue a philosophy of pacifism based upon the Bible. This is an unconscionable distortion of divine revelation.

Whether defensive or preemptive, war is a necessary component of divine justice when evil rears its ugly head. The Bible teaches us that all Christians have a God-given responsibility to take a stand against wickedness for our good and His glory. We have a responsibility to protect our families and possessions from murderers that would mock the laws of the God of the Bible and exalt themselves.

The misguided religious pacifist will argue, "How can you harmonize a call to arms with Jesus' blessings on meekness? And how can you support war given His commands to 'love our enemies' . . . to 'turn the other cheek' . . . and to 'return good for evil'?"

The answer is simple. In every case when Jesus admonished these virtuous attitudes, the issue was always the need for *a mortification of pride that inevitably seeks retaliation for personal offenses.* Jesus' passion was to call us to surrender our fanatical commitment to personal rights and vengeance and replace such attitudes with the love of Christ. Never do these admonitions apply to the very appropriate and necessary need for retaliation against criminal offenses and the military aggression of an evil enemy. In fact, war is an extension of capital punishment that God Himself instituted to maintain order and justice. This is well documented throughout Scripture.

We read in Genesis 9:6, "Whoever sheds man's blood, by man his blood shall be shed." And again in Exodus 21:12: "He who strikes a man so that he dies shall surely be put to death." Even in the New Testament Jesus restated this very principle in Matthew 26:52 when He condemned Peter for drawing his sword and cutting off the ear of the high priest's servant. There He said to Peter, "Put your sword back into its place; for all those who take up the sword shall perish by the sword." God even considers capital punishment (and its logical extension, war) as a *deterrent* to crime as indicated in Deuteronomy 17:13 where He warns, "Then all the people will hear and be afraid, and will not act presumptuously again."

I cannot imagine a world where fanatical extremists like Hitler, Stalin, Saddam Hussein, or Osama Bin Ladin are left unchecked. Meekness does not negate self-defense when a homicidal maniac attacks you or your family. Such reasoning is irrational. Gentleness does not mean we idly stand by and pray for peace when we are under assault. Love cannot exist without law, and law cannot exist without the sword. Scripture even affirms the importance of governments bearing the sword, claiming that government is "an avenger who brings wrath upon the one who practices evil"

(Romans 13:4). Indeed, there is "a time for war, and a time for peace" (Ecclesiastes 3:8).

I echo the sentiments of the line in a familiar song that says, "I'm proud to be an American!" and I do not believe for one minute that our country's greatness just happened by dumb luck. Rather, I am convinced that God has blessed and protected us because, at least in the past, we have honored Him as a nation. Likewise, we must honor those whom He has used as instruments of divine righteousness. The noble warriors of World War II, and specifically the sailors and Marines of the USS *Indianapolis*, are but samples of the past and present valor of our noble military personnel whom I, along with my father, seek to honor through his testimony. Together we pray that this story will be an encouragement to our military around the world and will ignite a fire of patriotism in every American.

As you read this harrowing true adventure, you will quickly see the power of faith and the undeniable hand of divine providence in the affairs of men and governments. You will see the crippling effects of sin in the ravages of war and the transforming power of the gospel of Christ in the hearts of men. You will see the metastasizing corruption of personal revenge and politics, even in our own military, that stooped to tactics of questionable integrity and succumbed to the temptations of injustice. But you will also rejoice in the victory of honor and honesty when a terrible wrong was righted because of the perseverance of those who would never stop fighting for truth. And certainly you will be deeply touched by the valor and humility of sailors and Marines who endured the unimaginable.

Finally, you will learn of a man, like many others, who truly loves his country, and his Savior and Lord, Jesus Christ. Without reservation I can say that there is no hypocrisy here. I have watched my father practice what he has preached. He has been my mentor and friend, and for this I am eternally grateful. Every fiber of his being is dedicated to Christ—validated by his love for my dear mother, all of his family, friends, and his shipmates of the USS *Indianapolis*.

But I must hasten to add, while the steel of his faith was forged in eternity past by a sovereign God, it was undoubtedly tempered in the fires of his adversity at sea. No man could possibly be the same after enduring such a crucible of grace. And it is my prayer, along with my father, that you too will never be the same after reading this story.

David Harrell

Chapter One

A Call to Arms

⚓

I said to the LORD,

"Thou art my God; Give ear, O LORD,

to the voice of my supplications.

O God the LORD, the strength of my salvation,

Thou hast covered my head in the day of battle."

Psalm 140:6-7

The Indianapolis *was the largest ship I had ever seen. Having grown up as a young boy during the depression in Chicago, seeing the magnificent ship was one of the greatest moments of my life. I hadn't ever seen a boat much bigger than a canoe for most of my life—the biggest thing I had seen was a barge some way offshore on Lake Michigan. Not only was the* Indianapolis *larger than this barge, but I got to see it sitting right there in the bay before me.*

Survivor Michael N. Kuryla Jr.

In San Francisco, we picked up big, big heavy boxes. They told us they were packages but didn't tell us what they were. Both of these packages were put into the port hangars. The morning we left San Francisco, it was very, very foggy. We pulled underneath the Golden Gate Bridge. I had driven over it many-a-time, but never under it. After we got out about seven miles, we started picking up speed. We could feel the vibrations from the fantail all the way to the front. The boilers were really taking off. We broke all speed records going to Pearl Harbor. The water was rough. My watch was the 5-inch gun on the quarter-deck, close to the packages. I used to sit on them or close by them on coils of rope. On watch we would take turns on the railing, watching over the side to see if we could see submarines or ships. You could see a ship about seven miles away.

Survivor Theodore M. Erickson

EVERY SURVIVOR OF WAR has a story to tell—stories of triumph and tragedy, faith and fear. Stories like mine, where fact is often stranger than fiction. Since that fateful night of July 30, 1945, when I stepped off a sinking ship into the unknown depths of the Pacific Ocean, there has never been a day when I have not reflected upon the horrors I experienced in the four and one-half days swimming in shark infested waters. However, while those frightening memories remain vivid in my mind's eye, one memory eclipses them all, namely, the unfailing presence of God that sustained me.

Luck had absolutely nothing to do with my survival. I believe with all my heart that it was solely by the providence of God that I lived through those dreadful days and nights. It is therefore to His glory that I recount my story—a story that exalts the One who ultimately authored it.

I am sure that in many ways my background is no different than hundreds of thousands of other folks who grew up in our great country during the years of the depression and survived the horrors of World War II. I suppose we all developed a survivor mindset in those days of adversity. As I reflect upon those bittersweet years of blood, sweat and tears mingled with the joys of family, friends and faith, I must confess that I wish our country could go back to those times and recapture the core values upon which our nation was founded—values originally shaped by our founding fathers who had an unshakable faith in the God of the Bible. Although the current moral freefall of America makes such a desire highly unlikely, perhaps my humble story will remind readers of the strength of character that was born out of that era and manifested in the millions of Americans who fought and died for our freedom.

Personal Preparations for War

I was born in a small house near the banks of the Tennessee River on October 10, 1924, in a little western Kentucky community called Turkey Creek. I was the oldest son of a family of two girls and seven boys. Descendants of the British Isles, we lived on a small farm where my dad was a hard-working farmer, carpenter, and when necessary, a schoolteacher. Mom was our best friend, with an amazing ability to provide for her family by cooking, sewing, helping in the garden, canning vegetables, caring for her henhouse, a husband and nine children.

Those were days of Spartan living, with few luxuries. Shoes came once a year from Sears Roebuck and, for the most part, we made our own toys. Life was simple back then: work or starve! But we were happy—an emotion few seem to experience these days. With their faith deeply rooted in the Lord Jesus Christ, my parents did all they knew to do to raise their children for the glory of God.

Prior to the Japanese attack on Pearl Harbor, my family and thousands of others across our great nation had no way of knowing that wicked men across the sea had our great country in their crosshairs. Little did we know that they even considered our safe little Kentucky farm part of a great spoil of war. I'm sure we took our freedom for granted in many ways; after all, freedom was all we had ever known. But by the time I was a junior in high school, the war in the Pacific was in full swing. With the decisive battle at Midway proving to be a turning point for the Allied forces in the Pacific, and convinced that my home and family were in imminent danger, I felt compelled to do my part by volunteering for the United States Marine Corps. In the fall of 1943, when the corn crop was "laid by," I went to the draft board and asked to join the Marines.

I remember well those days of duty and honor. I felt proud to serve my country, and even more honored to be able to protect my family and friends. As I listened to our old Silvertone radio, it sounded as though the Japanese were ready to storm the beaches of California. All of those Pacific islands seemed much closer in my limited and naïve comprehension, and I said to myself, "The

Japanese must be stopped!"

Years later I discovered that my simple-minded fear of the Japanese storming the coast of California was not as silly as it sounded. The Japanese commander that sunk the USS *Indianapolis* later revealed that one of their submarines actually launched a small-scale attack on California. In his book, *Sunk!*, Lieutenant Commander Mochitsura Hashimoto stated, "On February 24, 1942, submarine *I-17* penetrated the Santa Barbara Straits to the north of Los Angeles, and made the first submarine bombardment of America itself. The boat surfaced five minutes before sunset and fired rapidly at a target indicated by the captain at the periscope. There was evidence of panic on shore. Air-raid sirens were sounded. After firing ten rounds, *I-17* retired at high speed on the surface. En route she met an enemy destroyer hurrying to the scene of action, but slipped by unnoticed." 1.

Even if I had known of this small invasion, I really don't think it would have made much difference. I was convinced we were in danger and I was eager to volunteer for the task. This was a fight for freedom, a fight for survival, and a war where evil must be vanquished so justice and freedom could prevail. So, with the soul of a patriot and the heart of a warrior, I committed myself to the Marines. After having been sworn in at Indianapolis, Indiana, I was sent back to my home in Kentucky before reporting for duty.

Joining the service, or even being drafted, was an honorable undertaking in those days. We never heard of protesters, draft dodgers, or flag burners. When the war broke out, patriotism swelled in America. We willingly rationed clothes, food, fuel, and natural resources. It seemed that every able-bodied person was involved in working to defend America in some way or another. I remember my dad took me to the bus station and we said our good-byes. Dad was thirty-nine and I was nineteen. Leaving home wasn't easy. Not only was I leaving Mom and Dad, but two sisters and six brothers. What made it even worse was a certain young lady that had caught my eye one day at high school, a girl named Ola Mae Cathey. Four and a half years later, after the war, we were married and she has been my wife and life's companion since July 25, 1947.

The Fear of Death—Physical and Spiritual

During this time of preparation, the reality of war began to grip my soul and I began to view life differently. The likelihood of my death stirred my heart to reflect upon my own existence. I asked myself questions like, "Why was I placed here upon this earth? What is the real meaning of life? What if I don't make it back? Am I ready to stand before God and give an account of my life? What personal merit can I possibly offer God that would obligate Him to allow me into His holy presence for eternity? What have I really done with His Son the Lord Jesus Christ who died on a cross for my sins?"

I was absolutely convinced that God existed; any reasonable man can see that in creation. But, despite my external religious practices, highly acceptable in my "Bible Belt" culture, I knew that I had no real relationship with God. He was distant, not personal. I really had no faith, no passion to glorify God, no real hunger to hear the sound of His voice in Scripture and obediently serve Him, no real desire to commune with Him in prayer. And, having been exposed to His holy standard through my Christian upbringing, I knew that my best efforts fell far short. My conscience condemned me of not only my failure to honor God, but my *utter inability* to do so. I was scared. My fear of death in war suddenly paled into insignificance as I honestly examined my heart and saw my own wretchedness before God. My sin condemned me to an eternal hell, and I knew it. I needed mercy. I needed forgiveness. I needed a Savior.

Under profound conviction, the Lord, by His grace, drew me to Himself and gave me His gift of faith on the 1st day of August 1943 while I attended our little church in Murray, Kentucky. That Sunday after the sermon, the pastor gave an invitation and pronounced the benediction. Being deeply convicted that I had violated the laws of God in many ways, I remained seated as most everyone left. The pastor saw me and sat down by me and asked if he could help. I told him that I needed to get things right with the Lord and that I felt as if today was my last chance. He opened his Bible and turned to Acts 16:31, which says, "Believe in the Lord Jesus, and you shall be saved." He then reminded me that, "God who cannot lie has made you a promise. And if you will place your faith in Him as your Savior—the One who paid the penalty for your sins on a cross—He will save you." In the quietness of that moment, by the regenerating power of the Holy Spirit, I begged God for His gift of undeserved mercy and grace, based solely upon the atoning work of Jesus Christ. At that moment, "He delivered (me) from the domain of darkness, and transferred (me) to the kingdom of His beloved Son, in whom we have redemption, the forgiveness of sins" (Colossians 1:13).

It was on that day that God forgave me of my sins and I experienced the miracle of the new birth in Christ. As my burden of sin was finally laid at the foot of the cross, my heart was filled with joy and relief. I thought to myself, "Now I am ready for war, because now I am ready for eternity."

Soon I found myself enduring the rigors of boot camp in San Diego, California. Boot camp was tough and demanding, but I appreciated their commitment to see to it that we were well trained. They knew our lives would depend upon it. When I completed boot camp, I was sent to "Sea School" where I was later told that I would soon be assigned to a large combat ship. Somehow I knew then in my heart that God was up to something in my life far beyond my understanding. Far from the safety of my beloved Kentucky, I found myself alone in a world filled with dangerous unknowns, relieved only by the comforting truth of God's promise, "I will never leave thee, nor forsake thee . . . The Lord is my helper, and I will not fear what man shall do unto me" (Hebrews 13:5b, 6b, KJV). In March of 1944 I was assigned to the USS *Indianapolis*, and this was to be my home until her sinking on July 30, 1945.

The USS *Indianapolis* (CA-35)

The *Indianapolis* was a magnificent ship. Built for speed, her keel was laid down in Camden, New Jersey on March 31, 1930 by the New York Shipbuilding Corp. She was launched on November 7, 1931. After being properly fitted out for military service, she was then officially commissioned by the Navy in the Philadelphia Navy Yard on November 15, 1932.

One expert, Patrick J. Finneran, former Executive Director of the USS *Indianapolis* Survivors Memorial Organization, Inc., described the *Indy* as follows:

"From her inception, the *Indianapolis* was the pride of the Navy; representing as she did, all the very latest technology of her day. She was 610 feet, three inches in length, and sixty-six feet one inch at the beam (widest point). She drew seventeen feet six inches of draft (twenty-four feet when fully armed, manned and provisioned). Her design flank speed was thirty-two knots. She was equipped with eight White-Forster boilers located amidship, driving four Parsons geared turbines. Total horsepower was rated at 107,000, delivered through four screws. Her armament consisted of nine 8-inch guns placed in three turrets; two fore and one aft. Additionally there were four 5-inch guns, twenty-four 40 mm intermediate range guns and thirty-two 20 mm Oerlikon guns; the latter being installed during several overhauls and refits accomplished during the war." 2.

I still remember my first impression when I boarded the *Indy*, as she was affectionately called. My initial thought was, "This thing is big—real big!" It was like a floating city. It was an absolutely overwhelming experience for a country boy from Kentucky. My first sight of the massive guns gave me goose bumps. Never having seen guns larger than a double-barreled shotgun, I remember laughing to myself thinking, "My, my, my. We can win the war just by ourselves with these monsters!" Later I learned to operate both the 40 mm and the 5-inch guns. Since we had no foxholes in which to hide, I soon realized that our training and our ability were our only means of protection.

My sleeping quarters were small and hot. The bunks (or sleeping racks) were stacked three high. Of course new recruits got the top ones. They were a far cry from the feather bed I had been used to at home. But why complain? This was my new home and I was determined to make the best of it. I must admit, however, that I shed many a tear those lonely, homesick days and nights. I often poured out my heart to the Lord as I faced the unknowns of the future. Now, as a Marine, having been joined to a detachment of thirty-nine Marine officers and enlisted men, I knew that I had a job to do and a load to carry. I soon became an integral part of the *Indianapolis* crew. It was an honor to be part of "Ship's Company" of the *Indianapolis* that would eventually earn ten battle stars.

I was fascinated to learn that the *Indianapolis* had been chosen by President Roosevelt as his "Ship of State." Her speed and massive firepower truly captured the spirit of America. Given these impressive symbols of American power and honor, Roosevelt used her on numerous occasions to entertain royalty and great leaders from around the world as she frequently crossed the Atlantic and toured the great ports of South America.

The Mysterious Departure

Years after the war, I learned of some of the fascinating and mysterious history involving the *Indianapolis* that occurred just prior to the actual declaration of war that help set the stage for the story you are about to read. In April of 1940, when tensions concerning Japanese aggression began to mount, the U.S. fleet, including the *Indianapolis*, was moved from the west coast to Pearl Harbor, Hawaii. But just before the Japanese attack at Pearl Harbor, the *Indianapolis* was suspiciously removed from port, as if someone knew what was coming and wanted to protect her. To this day, these unexplained maneuverings remain shrouded in mystery. One historian writes:

"Officially, on the day the Japanese struck Pearl Harbor, December 7th, 1941, the *Indianapolis* was conveniently out of her home port, Pearl Harbor, making a simulated bombardment of Johnson Island off to the west. Captain E.W. Hanson, USN was then in command. It is noteworthy to mention here that all of the carriers assigned to Pearl were also conveniently out of Pearl as well. *Indianapolis* immediately joined Task Force 12 to search for the attacking Japanese carrier force. Returning to Pearl Harbor, the *Indianapolis* was assigned to Task Force 11 for operations against the enemy." 3.

Although we may never know with certainty the political and military machinations behind the scenes that resulted in the *Indy's* orders to leave Pearl Harbor just prior to the Japanese strike, we do know that it happened. Some have concluded that this is yet another piece of evidence validating the hypothesis that the American forces had prior knowledge of the attack. Certainly the implications of such a possibility are staggering given the loss of life that could possibly have been averted.

The following eyewitness account of Daniel E. Brady of the

V (Aviation) Division provides some fascinating insight into the mysterious exit and ultimate preservation of the *Indianapolis* on that fateful day.

"On December 5, 1941, I was a Seaman Second Class on board the heavy cruiser USS *Indianapolis* C A - 3 5. On that day, we were docked at the mine dock in Pearl Harbor. This was next to the submarine base, and across from 'Battleship Row.'

It was Friday afternoon, and as normal routine on weekends in port, all our married men and liberty sections were ashore, leaving approximately one third of the crew on board with the duty. Then, a surprising word was passed: 'The ship would get underway in one hour.'

'Impossible!' we commented among ourselves. Most of our crew were ashore and we could never recall them in time on such short notice. Soon, fifty marines in full battle gear came aboard, followed by forty or so civilian shipyard workers with their toolboxes. Next came truckloads of food and vegetables, which were dumped unceremoniously on the bleached, white, teakwood quarter-deck!

The quarter-deck was exclusively reserved for Admirals, Captains and ceremonial occasions. Why, we didn't even walk across it with our shoes on! This was blasphemy! What was going on?

Just as the word was given, we got underway in one hour's time without our crew and steamed out of Pearl Harbor. We traveled Friday night and Saturday with no word as to our destination. Sunday morning at about seven thirty we anchored at Johnson Island, a small island about 700 miles southwest of Hawaii. Hastily, we began unloading the Marines, civilians and stores. Then the word was passed: 'The Japs are bombing Pearl! This is no drill. Prepare the ship for battle action!'

Everything that could burn was thrown overboard. Lumber, paint, small boats, even President Roosevelt's great, ornate, bedroom suite he used when aboard the *Indy*. We then steamed back to Hawaiian waters and joined the old carrier, Lexington. After seven days and three attempts to enter Pearl, (Jap submarines were trying to sink the 'Lex' in the entrance), we finally made it, and could not believe what havoc had been wrought. We picked up our crew and survivors from the battleship Nevada and departed the following morning. To this very day, you cannot convince me that somebody didn't know this attack would take place.

Consider this: We were President Roosevelt's

favorite ship, and were also the flagship of Admiral Wilson Brown, head of Scouting Force, whose job it was to scout out and detect the enemy. And we were conveniently out of port at the time of the attack. Fate acts in funny ways at times. Being in the aviation unit, (Airdales), we usually disembarked our airplanes and their crews to Ford Island when we were in Pearl. This time (5 December 1941) our aircraft were kept aboard. Had they been at Ford Island they would have been destroyed!

After many years in the Pacific, I was transferred from the *Indy* before her tragic sinking, with the terrible loss of men—my shipmates, at the war's end." 4.

In some ways, it seems as though I have never left the *Indy*. Indeed, her story lives on even after all these years. Much mystery shrouds her story. Perhaps no other ship in wartime history has grabbed the interest of the American people like the *Indianapolis*. To her crew she was the queen of the fleet. Spared at Pearl, yet sacrificed for the cause at the deciding climax of WWII, the USS *Indianapolis* gave her all. As you will see, her fate stretches the limits of bad luck to their breaking point. There was something far greater at work, something supernatural, a force that orchestrated her every move, and continues to do so even now. But to her crew, she will always remain the queen of the Pacific fleet.

Chapter Two

The Indy Maru
⚓

To every thing there is a season, and a time to every purpose
under the heaven:
A time to be born, and a time to die;
a time to plant, and a time to pluck up that which is planted;
A time to kill, and a time to heal;
a time to break down, and a time to build up;
A time to weep, and a time to laugh;
a time to mourn, and a time to dance . . .
A time to love, and a time to hate;
a time of war, and a time of peace.
Ecclesiastes 3:1-4, 8 (KJV)

I have often felt that I had a unique navy experience being from Indiana and ending up on the USS Indianapolis! *. . . I participated in eight of the ten operations, the last being Okinawa. I am proud to have been a member of the crew that delivered the atomic bomb.*

Survivor Donald L. Beaty

As we entered the cabin, three men were already there. We saw two lead canisters, about knee-high, with long steel pipes through rings on top. As I made my way to the opposite side, I said, "This looks like it has to do with radiation." Silence. . . the two escorts, later identified as Captain Nolan and Major Furman, looked at each other, but said nothing. These canisters I was later told, contained the uranium-235 slugs which were used in the atomic bomb dropped on Hiroshima.

Survivor Richard A. Paroubek

WHILE THE WAR RAGED ACROSS THE SEA, the USS *Indianapolis* was being refitted with more sophisticated radar and gunnery equipment at Mare Island, San Francisco. My first duties as a Marine were on what we called "Goat Island" in the San Francisco area: guarding navy and marine personnel confined to the brig. Several weeks passed before I received my orders to board the USS *Indianapolis*, affectionately nicknamed *The Indy Maru*. Most ships were given nicknames, but it is not known how the *Indianapolis* got hers. It is interesting that "maru" is the Japanese word for "ship." 1.

I'll never forget that exhilarating day when we first sailed out of Mare Island in the early part of 1944. The reality that I was off to war really began to sink in. Little did I know the horrors that awaited me, nor the demonstration of divine providence that would see me through it all.

Our skipper was Capt. E.R. Johnson. I was proud to serve under him and naïvely excited as he set course for our first destination:

Pearl Harbor. There we were to "pick up our flag"—Navy talk for picking up an Admiral, ours being Admiral Raymond A. Spruance, Commander of the 5th fleet.

I can still remember the first time I saw Admiral Spruance walking on the forward deck of the *Indianapolis*. He did that often, and for long periods of time almost every day. I can only imagine the stress he had to endure given the enormity of his responsibilities. He was an impressive man that easily earned respect. He gave his young sailors and Marines confidence as we prepared for battle. We were all proud to serve under him.

Combat Aboard Ship

My first combat experience was at Kwajalein and Eniwetok in the Marshall Island chain. Our ultimate sights, however, were on Guam, Saipan and Tinian, crucial islands for providing a staging area for our new Boeing B-29 Superfortress bombers to be able to attack the mainland of Japan.

From the Marshalls we moved on to attack the Western Carolines. There our carrier planes struck the enemy at the Palau Islands where they bombed enemy airfields, sank three destroyers, seventeen freighters, five oilers and damaged another seventeen enemy ships. The Japanese lost 160 planes during these battles, with another forty-six destroyed on the ground. 2.

Fighting aboard the *Indy* was exhausting at times. In the Western Carolines we manned our guns for seventeen days straight in an effort to destroy the tremendous concrete tunnels and fortifications the Japanese had so effectively built. Tragically, our American forces lost approximately 7,000 men during the months of March and April of 1944 at Yap, Ulithi, Woleai and Palau. Although loss of life was high, these were strategic victories because they neutralized the enemy's ability to interfere with the U.S. landings on New Guinea, though some argued we would have been better off to have starved them out than gone in after them.

On the 13th of June, we moved on to the Marianas where the *Indianapolis* joined the pre-invasion bombardment group off Saipan. The Japanese were dug in deep on Saipan with their massive gun installations camouflaged and concealed behind trap doors on concrete bunkers. With the landing attack scheduled for June 15, Admiral Spruance maneuvered the *Indianapolis* in close enough to effectively superintend the attack, so close, in fact, that we experienced many near misses from the Japanese batteries. Fortunately, we were hit only one time by a defective shell that did not explode, causing only minor damage.

Under the cover of ferocious American bombardment, the 2nd and 3rd Marine Divisions launched their amphibious assault. They were met with stiff resistance when they came ashore. The well fortified Japanese bunkers were high above the beaches, capable of suddenly opening their massive trap doors, blasting our vulnerable boys below, and quickly concealing themselves again. The casualties for our marines were high. I experienced an almost overwhelming variety of emotions all at once that day, feeling everything from fear to fury. Not letting our emotions rule us, the crew of the *Indy* fought on with great discipline, doing all we could to support our vulnerable troops storming the beaches.

Desperate to relieve their beleaguered forces to the south in the Marianas, the Japanese launched a large fleet of battleships, carriers, cruisers and destroyers. Contrary to the deceptions of the Tokyo Rose propaganda that said that the Americans were running away from the massive flotilla of the Japanese Navy, Admiral Spruance ordered a fast carrier force to make haste to meet them head-on. A second force attacked their air bases at Iwo Jima and Chichi Jima in the Bonin and Volcano Islands. Admiral Spruance was confident of victory knowing that the U.S. had 104 ships of various kinds and 819 carrier-based planes available in the theater of operation. Estimates for the Japanese, however, indicated that they had suffered serious losses in the Pacific leaving them with only fifty-five ships and 430 planes. By then, the U.S. fleet had twice as many destroyers as the Japanese.

Our fleet met the enemy on June 19 in what was called the 'Battle of the Philippine Sea.' The Navy Department Naval History Division described the battle as follows:

"Enemy carrier planes, which hoped to use the airfields

of Guam and Tinian to refuel and rearm and attack our offshore shipping, were met by carrier planes and the guns of the escorting ships. That day the Navy destroyed 402 enemy planes while losing only seventeen of her own. (The) *Indianapolis*, which had operated with the force which struck Iwo Jima and Chichi Jima, shot down one torpedo plane. This famous day's work became known throughout the fleet as the "Marianas Turkey Shoot." With enemy air opposition wiped out, the U.S. carrier planes pursued and sank two enemy carriers, two destroyers, and one tanker and inflicted severe damage on other ships." 3.

Kamikaze Planes and the Insanity of War

Whenever I reflect on these battles, especially the "Marianas Turkey Shoot," I find myself shaking my head in dismay at the insanity of war. The suicide missions of the Japanese kamikaze pilots serve as a perfect illustration. What a colossal waste of lives and resources—and for what? With an economy of words, God gives us the answer. "What is the source of quarrels and conflicts among you? Is not the source your pleasures that wage war in your members? You lust and do not have; so you commit murder. And you are envious and cannot obtain; so you fight and quarrel" (James 4:1-2).

Most of the Japanese soldiers, especially the officers, considered their emperor a god and worshipped him. They considered it an honor to die for him. Likewise, most Japanese considered themselves Shintoists (belonging to the religion of Shintoism, primarily a mystical religious system of nature and ancestor worship). This deceptive belief system was so powerful that it inspired their soldiers to make banzai suicide attacks as an act of religious service. Capture was considered a profound disgrace upon their families who considered those captured as dead. For this reason they would rather die than be taken prisoner by the enemy. With such fanaticism, one can only imagine the staggering loss of life had we not later used the atomic bombs and invaded Japan instead.

As Japan's war machine began to fall apart, their desperation gave birth to the concept of suicide planes called *kamikaze*, meaning *divine wind*. (They also used human torpedoes called *kaitens*). With their planes loaded with explosives and only enough fuel to make it to their designated target, kamikaze pilots would ceremonially step into their cockpits for the last time with feelings of great pride and fly off to their death.

I remember feeling pity for the ones we shot down and rescued. Most of them were poorly trained young pilots, blinded by a warped sense of patriotism, honor, and, like all suicide warriors, a fanatical religious fervor to serve some phantom god (or gods) that do not exist. I was intrigued to watch them as we lifted them out of the sea onto the deck of the *Indy*. Wounded and scared, I can still see their white, pajama-like death uniforms and their young faces overwhelmed with terror and confusion. After dressing their wounds and conducting the customary interrogations, we would transfer them to other ships as prisoners of war.

After the "Marianas Turkey Shoot," the *Indianapolis* returned to Saipan in June to resume fire support for six days. We then moved on to Tinian to blast shore installations. Meanwhile, Guam had been taken, and the *Indianapolis* was the first ship to enter Apra Harbor (previously an American base) since it had been captured by the Japanese early in the war.

For the next few weeks we operated in the Marianas area and then proceeded to the Western Carolines where further landing assaults were planned. From September 12 through 29, both before and after our landings, we bombarded the Island of Peleliu in the Palau Group. We then went on to operate for ten days around the island of Manus in the Admiralty Islands before returning back to San Francisco to the Mare Island Navy Yard for repairs and maintenance. 4.

New Skipper Comes Aboard

In December 1944 we welcomed our new skipper, Capt. Charles B. McVay III. Unlike Captain Johnson, who was all business in his military demeanor, Capt. McVay was more personable and enjoyed interacting with the men on a relational level. Johnson ran a very tight ship requiring many drills and "General Quarters" (i.e. battle ready) early in the morning. McVay, on the other hand, ran a looser ship, not requiring us to be battle ready all the time, nor did he expect us to keep watertight doors closed and dogged when we were in forward areas. However, I never thought of him as being lax in any way.

I served as a marine orderly for both of these fine captains and had a bit of a firsthand experience with them. I still laugh as I recall driving Capt. Johnson down to the Navy Yard one sunny day. He was just as much in charge of that jeep as he was the *Indy*, except on that occasion I was at the controls and the fine Captain was in the backseat telling me how to drive.

With Capt. McVay now at the helm of the *Indy*, and our overhaul at Mare Island complete, we joined Vice Adm. Marc Mitscher's carrier task force on the 14th of February 1945. There we played a vital support role as our forces attacked the installations in the Home Islands of Japan itself. The *Indy* gave its support to the first air strikes on Tokyo since General Doolittle's invasion in April of 1942, preparing the way for the bloody struggles at the landings on Iwo Jima. 5.

The campaign around the Home Islands stands out in my mind. It was crucial for us to gain tactical surprise and we did so by traversing the Alutian Island chain in terrible weather. I remember several occasions where I was at watch on the bridge during high seas. As the ship forged ahead, the bow would descend into the great valleys of water, then plow into the frigid banks of the oncoming waves causing a sleet-like spray to strike me with stinging force.

Our mission was successful in the Home Islands campaign. Between February 14 and 17, the Navy lost forty-nine carrier planes while shooting down or destroying 499 enemy planes. Our task force sank one Japanese carrier, nine coastal ships, two destroyer escorts and a cargo ship. While this was going on, Japan was being systematically devastated every day by our air force. 6.

Iwo Jima

With their homeland under attack and their war machine gradually being diminished, desperation caused the Japanese to fight with a zealous determination. They fiercely defended Iwo Jima, proving to be one of the toughest of all the islands for the United States to secure. It was estimated that approximately 21,000 Japanese troops inhabited the labyrinth of coral tunnels on the volcanic island. The *Indy's* mission was simple; bombard them! We had the ability to fire over 500 rounds of 5-inch gun ammunition in under six minutes, sending massive amounts of destructive flak as far as eight miles. The big 8-inch guns could lob 250-pound shells up to eighteen miles. The concussion from the 8-inchers was staggering. In fact, their enormous recoil would actually move the massive

Indianapolis sideways in the water. We were also well equipped for close range warfare with the firepower of our 40 mm and 20 mm deck guns. They were especially effective on kamikaze planes

Torpedo suicide planes were also a persistent threat to our ships. I will never forget the day when one flew in low and horizontal, trying to make its way across our bow. As always, our mission was to shoot him before he could get to us. That particular day I was a fuse box loader on one of the 5-inch guns. I would place a seventy-five-pound shell into a fuse box hitched up to what was called "sky aft radar." This radar system would then relay the actual coordinates of the incoming enemy plane to the shell itself, instructing it to explode its flak precisely in front of the plane.

As the plane came roaring by from left to right, the 5-inch gun immediately to the left of my gun continued firing in its left to right range of motion until its rotation was complete. With its muzzle now approximately sixteen feet from where I stood, pointed as far forward as possible toward the bow of the ship, it fired again. The concussion of the blast was so powerful that it knocked me to the deck while I was still holding the seventy-five-pound shell. The force of the explosion dislodged my cotton earplugs causing them to fall out and quickly blow away in the Pacific wind. Though dazed by the detonation, God enabled me to get to my feet and load the shell. As it fired, the percussion of the blasts further damaged my unprotected ears causing temporary deafness and blood to run out of my left ear. While our efforts averted the enemy plane and our lives were spared, I permanently suffered a fifty percent loss of hearing in that ear.

Okinawa

By March 4, 1945 we joined the pre-invasion bombardment of Okinawa where we fired 8-inch shells into the Japanese beach defenses. We soon discovered that our 8-inch projectiles were glancing off the concrete pillboxes like ricocheting bullets. This required us to move out further and thus lob the shells over and down on our targets—a strategy that proved most successful. In the seven days of fighting at Okinawa, the crew of the *Indy* shot down six planes and assisted in splashing two others.

One morning in particular stands out to me. The ship's lookouts spotted a single-engine Japanese kamikaze fighter plane diving vertically directly at the ship's bridge. We immediately opened fire with our 20 mm guns. Although we hit the plane and caused it to swerve, the pilot was still able to release his bomb at the last second and crash his plane on the port side of the after main deck. The plane toppled off the ship and fell into the sea causing little damage to the surface of the ship. The bomb, on the other hand, tore through the deck armor, the mess hall, the berthing compartment below and the fuel tanks in the lowest chambers before crashing through the bottom of the ship and exploding in the water underneath us. It was a miracle that we only suffered moderate damage.

The official naval report indicated "the concussion blew two gaping holes in the ship bottom and flooded compartments in the area, killing nine crewmen. Although the *Indianapolis* settled slightly by the stern and listed to port, there was no progressive flooding; and the plucky cruiser steamed to a salvage ship for emergency repairs. Here, inspection revealed that her propeller shafts were damaged, her fuel tanks ruptured, her water-distilling equipment ruined; nevertheless, the battle-proud cruiser made the long trip across the Pacific to the Mare Island Navy Yard under her own power." 7.

Surprise Combat Orders

It was a relief to come back to Mare Island and leave the Pacific front. The break from combat was welcome but short-lived. Suddenly, while at Hunters Point in San Francisco, we received word that all leaves were cancelled. Despite the fact that the *Indy* was not fully repaired and tested, we were ordered to get underway immediately. Not knowing what was going on, we boarded and quickly followed orders as we loaded last-minute provisions.

There was an obvious tension in the air—a mood of excitement combined with confusion and secrecy. Everyone knew that something special was going down but no one knew what. The place was crawling with marine guards and top military brass. My curiosity was fueled even more when my Marine Captain Parke ordered me to station guards around the mysterious cargo that had been brought aboard. A large crate, measuring about five feet high, five feet wide, and perhaps fifteen feet in length was hoisted onto the port hangar off the quarter-deck—an area normally used to store, catapult and retrieve small observation airplanes.

The plywood crate had been lashed down onto the deck with large straps fastened by countersunk screws. Each countersunk void was filled with a red wax seal to serve as a tamper indicator. After stationing guards around the mysterious container, I immediately proceeded to obey my orders and do the same for another curious piece of cargo brought aboard and placed in a compartment on the upper deck reserved strictly for officers.

There I stationed a guard outside one of Admiral Spruance's unused rooms, since he was not on board at the time. Inside the room was an ominous-looking black metal canister that a couple of sailors had brought on board dangling from a metal pole hoisted upon their shoulders. The cylinder was about two feet long and maybe eighteen inches wide and was padlocked in a steel cage that had been welded securely to the deck floor. A new boarder by the name of Captain Nolan had the key to the padlock. Adding to the suspense, the crew was warned that whatever happened in the days to come, *that canister must not be lost or destroyed.* Whatever it contained was obviously of enormous importance. I later discovered that when the black canister was aboard the transport plane, it had its very own parachute, just in case something went wrong.

Captain Nolan and another Army officer who boarded with him, a Major Robert Furman, remained with the secret cargo. They seemed conspicuously nervous and out of place, and stayed to themselves in the days that followed. Weeks later we discovered that they were not military officers at all, but rather two scientists in disguise from the top-secret weapons labs in Los Alamos, New Mexico. We also later learned that our cargo consisted of the integral components of the atomic bombs that would be dropped twenty-one days later on Hiroshima and Nagasaki, code named, "Little Boy" and "Fat Man."

The ominous canister contained uranium-235, accounting for approximately half the fissionable material possessed by the United States, valued around $300 million. According to one historian, "the contents of the crate were known to only a handful of people: President Truman and Winston Churchill; Robert Oppenheimer and his closest colleagues at the Manhattan Project; and Captain James Nolan and Major Robert Furman, who were now aboard the *Indy*. In reality, Nolan was a radiologist and Furman an engineer engaged in top-secret weapons intelligence." 8.

Full Speed Ahead—A Record Run

On July 16, 1945 at 8:30 A.M. we exited San Francisco Bay and set sail for Pearl Harbor, Hawaii. Although I do not remember, it is said that the *Indy* actually paused soon after leaving the wharf to await the final results of the Trinity Test that had just been completed in Los Alamos, New Mexico. Evidently, had the bomb malfunctioned, we would have been instructed to return to our mooring. Obviously, the test was a success, so we made our way to the open seas.

Being one of the fastest ships in the Navy, the *Indianapolis* made record time, covering 2,405 miles in only seventy-four and a half hours. After only six hours of taking on supplies and fuel, we left Pearl Harbor and immediately raced unescorted to the island of Tinian, arriving there on July 26. In total, the *Indianapolis* had set a record in covering some 5,300 miles from San Francisco to our B-29 base in Tinian in only ten days. 9.

Tinian Island is a small island along the Marianas Trench, 100 nautical miles north of Guam Island, approximately twelve miles in length and six miles in width. Its proximity to Japan made it a strategic B-29 Superfortress airbase. The four runways of the north field had been extended to a length of 8,500 feet providing the necessary runway to accommodate gigantic aircraft burdened with heavy bombs and extra fuel needed to complete nightly twelve-hour round trip raids on Japan.

Although our bombing raids were having a devastating impact on the enemy, Washington had made plans to invade Japan with two operations involving over two million American soldiers. Under the code name Olympic, 800,000 troops were to go ashore on the southern island of Kyushu in November, with a second amphibious assault called Coronet to land on the island of Honshu near Tokyo in April of 1946.

None of us aboard the *Indianapolis* had any idea that the mysterious cargo we had just unloaded at Tinian would make all these plans unnecessary. None of us knew that we had just delivered the most devastating weapon in the history of the world. None of us knew that God was using the crew of the *Indianapolis* to accomplish His purposes in bringing the war to an abrupt and terrifying end. And certainly, none of us knew that four days after arriving in Tinian our beloved *Indy Maru,* and most of her crew, would be lost at sea.

Chapter Three

Tragedy Explodes—
the First Day

⚓

Those who go down to the sea in ships,

Who do business on great waters;

They have seen the works of the LORD,

And His wonders in the deep.

For He spoke and raised up a stormy wind,

Which lifted up the waves of the sea.

They rose up to the heavens, they went down to the depths;

Their soul melted away in their misery.

They reeled and staggered like a drunken man,

And were at their wits' end.

Then they cried to the LORD in their trouble,

And He brought them out of their distresses.

He caused the storm to be still, so that the waves of the sea

were hushed.

Then they were glad because they were quiet,

So He guided them to their desired haven.

Let them give thanks to the LORD for His lovingkindness,

And for His wonders to the sons of men!

Let them extol Him also in the congregation of the people,

And praise Him at the seat of the elders.

Psalm 107:23-32

My last view of the Indianapolis *was bow down, flag still flying on*
the stern, and men jumping into the turning screws. Their screams
still haunt me today.

Survivor John (Jack) C. Slankard

What a shock—beyond belief! I had been comfortably asleep on the
signal bridge deck just fifteen or so minutes prior, and now my ship
was gone. I was in the ocean among very large white capping
swells, all wet, covered with smelly fuel oil and hearing distant
cries for help coming out of the darkness.

Survivor Paul W. McGinnis

The night was one of terror. Fighting broke out. Demented men were
victims of shark fear—everyone became the enemy. One shouted,
"There's Japanese on this line," and all hell broke loose—men were
stabbing the people next to them, fighting with whoever was close.
Toward morning it became quiet. I guess those of us who remained
became exhausted to a point of no return. This was our last hurrah.
Less than one hundred men left out of four hundred, and some with
their faces down on the water . . . more dead than alive.

Survivor Frank J. Centazzo

The first thing that was so horrible was the fuel oil that covered the
water. Every breath I took made me so sick I vomited everything I
had in my stomach. We were all black from the fuel oil covering our

bodies. We did what we had to do to survive the ordeal at sea. I never gave up hope.

Survivor Maurice G. Bell

I reached the boat deck aft, the ship had already heeled over forty degrees. There was that ominous groaning and grating of metal, which is the death rattle of a ship breaking up. We had no communication with the bridge. Shells from our deck guns were bouncing around the deck like tenpins. Their fuses were set and I kept expecting one to go off. We kept tossing them overboard until I knew the ship was doomed. I ordered the men around me to abandon ship.

Survivor Clarence U. Benton

Shortly after midnight, I woke up when the torpedo hit and climbed out on the deck. My feet were burned when I hit the deck and I did not know what was going on . . . Men were screaming all around and many were wounded. The ship listed to one side and I went into the ocean. After landing in the water, one of the planes started to roll over on me and another sailor. We finally got away from it. When we looked up we could see the Indy *in the distance, plowing through the water on its side. The sky was all lit up with fire as it finally rolled over. I saw men on top and the screws were still turning as it went straight down.*

Survivor John T. Heller

WE NEVER KNOW WHAT A NEW DAY WILL BRING. As a Christian, I have learned that even my most carefully made plans are ultimately subservient to a sovereign God that "causes all things to work together for good to those who love God, to those who are called according to His purpose" (Romans 8:28). Indeed, "the mind of man plans his way, but the LORD directs his steps" (Proverbs 16:9). What happened next to all of us on board the USS *Indianapolis* was a life-changing event that none of us could have anticipated. And none who survived were ever the same.

With our top-secret cargo now safely delivered to the B-29 base at Tinian, we were ordered to first proceed 120 miles south to Guam and later to sail on to Leyte to meet up with the battleship USS *Idaho* for seventeen days of drills. There we would be familiarized with new equipment and conduct gunnery practice with a partially new crew in urgent need of training. We would also get prepared to participate in the invasion of Kyushu, one of Japan's southernmost islands. Overall, this journey was a dangerous 1,300-mile jaunt that would take us out of the Marianas Sea Frontier and into the Philippine Sea Frontier. Since the *Indy* had no sonar gear to detect enemy submarines—a task relegated to destroyers—Captain McVay was concerned about our vulnerability. 1.

On July 27 we arrived in Guam, home of the command center for the Pacific war theater known as CINPAC. Captain McVay was still concerned about the probability of Japanese submarines lurking about in the remote waters we were about to traverse, so he asked for a destroyer escort for added protection. His request was denied. The command intelligence report from CINPAC headquarters insisted the waters were safe. 2.

Unfortunately, the report withheld some essential information. In an effort to maintain the secrecy of their ability to decipher encrypted Japanese command messages through an ingenious top-secret code-breaking program called ULTRA, the U.S. command maintained a policy to randomly withhold precise enemy ship locations from Navy captains. This allowed some Japanese ships to avoid being attacked, giving them the impression that we had not broken their code and thereby avoiding the possibility of them changing their encryption codes and making our deciphering system obsolete. 3.

In light of this policy, CINPAC intelligence withheld two relevant pieces of information from McVay. First, they failed to mention that the Japanese Tamon submarine group had been patrolling our anticipated route. Second, they did not tell McVay that on July 24, just three days prior to the *Indy's* arrival in Tinian, a destroyer escort, the USS *Underhill* had been sunk by a kaiten (a manned suicide torpedo) released from a large Japanese patrol sub on the same route we would be navigating to Leyte. 4.

Traversing the Unknown

Vulnerable, unescorted and uninformed, the *Indy* left the safety of the Mariana Seas and entered the vast unknowns of the Philippine Sea Frontier. Life aboard ship was relaxed for the crew as we went about our daily operations. Of course we knew nothing of the skipper's concerns about our vulnerability.

The temperature was a tropical 110 degrees during the day—hot and muggy. Our marine compartment below deck was an oven at night, somewhere around ninety degrees. Although air was pumped into the cramped chambers, it still felt like a sauna, making it almost impossible for any of us to sleep at night. The temperature in the engine rooms usually exceeded 120 degrees, even with all the hatches and doors opened to draw in any outside breeze. For this reason we were given permission to sleep topside on the open deck. Each of us would search for an open space to spread out our blankets so we could enjoy our designated four hours of sleep.

We were traveling in what was called "Yoke Modified" position, denoting a more relaxed state of sailing. This was a normal status for waters perceived to be safe from enemy attack. Our battle-ready state was known as "Condition Able." This meant that we were on watch for four hours then off for four hours—an exhausting schedule that left little time for sleep and rest. Had we been apprised of the danger that lay ahead, we would have traveled at the most secure position where all hatches and doors would have been dogged and sealed off, making passage very limited, a position known as "Zed."

It is only human to reflect on that fateful night and play the "What if . . ." game. Certainly there was a high probability that things would have turned out much differently had we been properly informed and prepared. But that is all history now. Everything unfolded according to God's intended plan and for His purposes. We were traveling according to the fallacious conditions and instructions outlined for us at CINPAC—good reason for the ultimate blame for the ensuing tragedy to have been placed on the high command of the Navy.

On the night of July 29, the sea was relatively calm with overcast skies. Captain McVay agreed to cease the presumably defensive zigzag maneuver thought to create a more evasive target—a naval regulation later proven to be ineffective. Lieutenant McKissick took the watch on the bridge at 6:00 P.M. 5. The ship was on course 262 True, which was due west. Noting the overcast skies, Captain McVay entered the bridge and said to McKissick, "You may secure from zigzagging after twilight." McKissick responded,

"Aye, aye, sir." And steadily the *Indy* continued on to her destiny. 6.

I got off watch around midnight and decided to grab my blanket from my locker below and sleep topside on the breezy deck. The night before, I stretched the regulations a bit and slept on top of number one turret in a large life raft. A marine buddy by the name of Munson had the same idea and joined me there. But on this night, not wanting to risk losing any of my hard-earned stripes, I chose instead to sleep on the open deck under the barrels of number one turret.

The *Indy* was cruising through the waters at about seventeen knots. Her large engines, combined with the sound of her wake, droned a familiar lullaby. Tired and homesick, and missing my family and my little brunette back home, I wrapped my blanket around me and curled up on the steel deck hoping for a few hours of rest. After thanking the Lord for His provision and protection thus far, I asked Him to watch over my loved ones back in Kentucky. Then, using the arch of my shoe for a pillow, I drifted off to sleep.

Enemy in Wait

There has not been a season in my life since that night that I fail to remember what happened next. I had innocently fallen asleep in harm's way, utterly unaware that the Japanese submarine *I-58*, under the command of Lieutenant Commander Mochitsura

Hashimoto, had been silently slithering through the dark sea with its serpentine periscope and had spotted us at about 11:00 P.M.

The *I-58* was a formidable submarine measuring 356 feet in length. Although the normal safe diving depth for Japanese submarines was 300 feet, the *I-58* was designed to go even deeper to evade their enemies, capable of descending to 450 feet. 7. It had been commissioned in September 1944, and carried a crew of 105 officers and men. 8.

It was part of the celebrated Tamon group—one of six submarines left in the dwindling Japanese fleet. She was powered by two 4,700-horsepower diesel engines capable of gliding submerged through the water at seventeen knots and could travel 21,000 miles before refueling. Commander Hashimoto had in his arsenal nineteen torpedoes and six kaitens (which means "the turn toward heaven") complete with twelve suicide warriors since each kaiten required a two-man crew. 9. Each kaiten weighed about eight tons and contained powerful explosive warheads. Their estimated top speed was about twenty knots and they were capable of travel-ing a distance of around twenty-seven miles. Fanatical kaiten pilots were always ready to climb inside and steer themselves into glory—unless they missed, as was often the case. Since they were not recoverable, they would simply run out of fuel and silently sink to the ocean floor where both man and machine would be crushed by the enormous pressure. 10.

The *I-58* had just been fitted with two new kinds of radar

equipment, one for detecting surface ships and one for detecting aircraft. The sub was also well equipped with both electronic and acoustic sonar. Since they were also armed with six kaitens, the open deck had been stripped to only one 25 mm machine gun. 11.

Commander Hashimoto had been at sea for four years and had yet to destroy an enemy ship. He was desperate for a kill. Now he had his chance. The noble *Indianapolis* was an easy target as she unwittingly made her way into the crosshairs of Hashimoto's periscope. According to the testimony of Hashimoto given many months later, no kaitens were needed—a disappointment for the twelve kaiten crewmembers who wanted to be launched. The exhilaration of a possible "first kill" combined with the anxiety of engaging the enemy caused tension to run high aboard the *I-58*. In his book, *Sunk!*, Commander Hashimoto describes what happened after his navigator shouted, "Bearing red nine-zero degrees, a possible enemy ship." 12.

As soon as we were fully submerged I gave the orders: "Ship in sight," "All tubes to the ready," "Kaitens stand by." It was 11:08 p.m. After diving we had altered course to port and the black shape was now right ahead . . . Gradually the supposed enemy seemed to be getting closer. We were ready to give a salvo of six torpedoes. The dark shape continued on a course which was bringing it straight toward us. Was it a destroyer coming on for a depth-charge attack, having already detected our existence? Even if it was not, it would be difficult to score a torpedo hit if it came straight on over the top of us. I had some bad moments when thinking it might be a destroyer. . . We couldn't estimate the range since we didn't know the class of ship. We couldn't yet hear anything on the hydrophones. The round black spot gradually became triangular in shape. The time was 11:09 p.m. "Six torpedoes will be fired." I decided to fire from all tubes in one salvo. At the same time I ordered the crew of Kaiten 6 to embark and Number 5 to stand by.

The target began to assume the appearance of a large warship, and the uppermost part of the triangular black spot had resolved itself into two portions. There was a large mast forward. We've got her, I thought. The fact that the enemy was now visible in two distinct portions made it less likely that she would pass right over us, and the class of ship was now apparent. I was able to assess the masthead height as ninety feet. She was either a battleship or large cruiser. The range fell to four thousand yards. The expected range at time of firing—two thousand yards—and the bearing—green forty-five degrees—were set. A hydrophone report gave the enemy speed as moderately high. I used this estimate for the moment, but visual observation didn't put it so high, and I altered the setting to twenty knots. As for the Kaitens, I had been so occupied with the ordinary torpedoes that I hadn't given the orders for standing by to launch though the Kaiten crews kept coming to ask about it. A Kaiten attack at this stage of the moon would be difficult and I determined not to use them unless the ordinary torpedo attack failed.

We had the moon behind us and the enemy ship was now clearly visible. She had two turrets aft and a large tower mast. I took her to be an *Idaho*-class battleship. The crew were all agog, awaiting the order to fire the torpedoes. All was dead quiet . . . The favorable moment for firing was approaching. I altered the setting of the director to green sixty degrees, range fifteen hundred yards, and began the approach for firing. At last, in a loud voice, I gave the order, "Stand by—Fire!" the torpedo-release switch pressed at intervals of two seconds and then the report came from the torpedo room, "All tubes fired and correct." Six torpedoes were speeding, fanwise, toward the enemy ship. I took a quick look through the periscope, but there was nothing else in sight. Bringing the boat on to a course parallel with the enemy, we waited anxiously. Every minute seemed an age. Then on the starboard side of the enemy by the forward turret, and then by the after turret there rose columns of water, to be followed immediately by flashes of bright red flame. Then another column of water rose from alongside Number 2 turret and seemed to envelop the whole ship—"A hit, a hit!" I shouted as each torpedo struck home, and the crew danced round with joy. There was still nothing else in sight and the enemy was stopped but still afloat. I raised the day periscope and gave the conning-tower crew a sight. Soon came the sound of a heavy explosion, far greater than that of the actual hits. Three more heavy explosions followed in quick succession, then six more. The crew, not realizing the cause, were shouting, "Depth-charge attack," so I hastily reassured them that it was our target exploding and that there was no other enemy in sight. I saw several flashes aboard the enemy, but she showed no signs of sinking. I therefore stood by to give her a second salvo. From the Kaitens came the cry, "Since the enemy won't sink, send us." The enemy certainly presented an easy target for them in spite of the dark, but what if she should sink before the Kaitens reached her? Once launched they were gone for good, and it seemed a pity to risk wasting them. I therefore decided not to use them this time.

As soon as reloading was completed, we surfaced and raised periscope only to find there was nothing to be seen. I made for the spot where I thought she would have sunk, but still couldn't see anything. However, it was over an hour since the first action and I was certain now that she had sunk. A ship so damaged could not have got away at high speed. Even had she got away she would still have been in sight. I wanted, however, some proof that she had definitely sunk, but it was difficult to spot any flotsam in the darkness. With feelings of regret I made off to the northeast for fear of reprisals from ships or aircraft which might have been in company with our late enemy, and after running on the surface for an hour we dived to prepare for the next encounter. The ship we had sunk turned out to be the *Indianapolis*. 13.

Ambushed at Sea

As Hashimoto indicated, the first torpedo pierced the *Indy* on the forward starboard side about forty feet in front of number one turret where I slept. The concussion jarred me instantly to my feet. In the amount of time it took Commander Hashimoto to say, "fire one . . . fire two," the second torpedo hit around midship, forward of the quarter-deck, somewhere in the close vicinity of my marine compartment. Then, a few seconds later, a third explosion rocked the ship. It was the ammunition magazine underneath me. The explosion blew all the way through the top of number one turret—my bed the night before and Munson's bed that disastrous night. I'm sure he never felt a thing. The detonations sent water high into the air, drenching me as it rained down and protecting me from the massive fireball that flared all around me. The blast was so powerful that the massive turret with its three eighteen-foot barrels was lifted completely off its moorings and set over to the starboard side.

I was stunned and confused. No one was firing at us and we were not firing at anyone. I couldn't understand what was going on. I looked toward the front of the ship, and to my astonishment, it was gone! Approximately thirty-five feet of the bow had disappeared. It had been completely cut off. I then realized what had happened. We had been torpedoed.

Below deck, beneath me, I could hear and feel the bulkheads breaking under the pressure of the water as the *Indy*'s gigantic screws continued to push her forward. Massive fires from the explosions lit up the night sky, exposing the doomed *Indianapolis* to any enemy that could still be lurking nearby. All electrical power had been cut off. All communications had also been rendered inoperative. As a result, no word was sent to the engine room to stop the engines. Within a minute of the initial blast, I had come to my senses and knew the ship was going to sink. The open bow of the ship was already going under water.

I immediately made my way back to my emergency station, which was midship on the quarter-deck. As I did, men were coming up from below deck screaming from excruciating pain. Most were in their night skivvies and had been blown out of their bunks. Hysterically they cried for help. Many had scorched flesh literally hanging from their faces and arms. The pungent smell of burning flesh and hair was nauseating. Compound fractures revealed protruding bones from the bodies of those who had been blown up against the bulkhead walls. It was a living hell. I'll never forget the fires, the horrified faces and the cacophony of screams. I can still hear the explosions and the screeching metal being twisted and torn by the tons of water the ship was taking on.

On the way to my emergency station, I noticed the ship was already listing about twenty degrees to the starboard. Evidently, the second explosion had made a gaping hole in the starboard side, flooding most of the compartments in the forward area. As bulkheads continued to break, more and more water filled the lower compartments causing the ship to actually erect itself for a minute or so. But as she continued to plow forward and bulkheads gave way, the ship began to roll severely to starboard. Because of CINPAC's unwillingness to warn us of the high probability of imminent danger, we had been traveling completely open. Battle-ready status had been discouraged. Watertight doors were not closed and dogged. As unthinkable as it may be, the gallant *Indianapolis* and her noble crew had become victims not only of the enemy, but of the very Navy they served.

As best I can recall amidst all the chaos, it took me about four minutes to get to my emergency station. Realizing my life jacket was in the fiery inferno below deck in my locker, I was eager to get to my station where I knew many more were located. When I got there, I could see the canvas bags filled with jackets hanging all around on the open bulkheads. I yelled over to Lt. Stauffer, "Sir, permission to cut down the life jackets!" Committed to following Navy procedures, he quickly retorted, "No! Not until we are given orders to abandon ship!"

Suddenly, a navy commander I recognized came from below deck—Commander Lipski. He was burned severely and pleading for help. At the sight of this, someone cried out, "Get the commander a life jacket!" Immediately a sailor cut down the canvas bags filled with kapok life vests. As they tumbled to the deck, I quickly grabbed one and put it on. I decided not to fasten it in the straddle, contemplating the jump I would soon have to make into the sea. Other sailors likewise scrambled for a jacket, each man knowing they were about to face the challenge of the great deep and perhaps soon face their Creator and Judge. A controlled panic could be seen on every face. The icy grip of fear nearly paralyzed every young sailor and Marine. Our faces betrayed the terror of the unknown as we suddenly found ourselves confronted with the very thing every human being hates—utter helplessness. Even so, the will to survive fortified itself with the face of bravery as we all desperately prepared to leap into the pitch-black water.

Another two or three minutes passed before word of mouth spread that Captain McVay had given the word to abandon ship. He had been waiting for a damage control report, but tragically, those who had gone below to make that assessment never made it back topside.

By now men were being washed overboard. The front half of

the ship was completely underwater. It was nearly impossible to stand on the open deck because of her severe list to starboard. When word to abandon ship finally reached the quarter-deck, many men ran to the high side (port side) and began jumping off. It was bedlam. In the light of the flames I could see men jumping on top of each other. I recall making my way to the port side and hanging on to the rail to keep from falling due to the steep incline. As I stood there, I looked out into the blackness of night and then looked at the pitch-black oil floating on top of the water below. I will never forget that moment. It is indelibly etched in my mind. The stark reality of what was really happening flooded my senses in a torrent of horror. I was suddenly face to face with my mortality. Eternity was before me. And in the midst of my fear and utter helplessness, I cried out to God in prayer.

Anyone who has ever experienced a similar situation will understand what I am about to say: there are times when you pray, then there are times when you *pray*! This was one of those latter times. No one offered to help me because no one else *could* help me. I was there alone—or so it seemed. But as I reached out in desperation to the Savior of my soul, He suddenly made it clear to me that He was also going to be the Savior of my life. There was no audible voice. Something far more comforting was suddenly given to me. An unexplainable and ineffable peace enveloped me like a warm blanket on a frosty night. With the undeniable marks of the supernatural, the chill of terror was replaced with the glowing warmth of divine assurance. I knew within my heart that God was answering my prayers and was going to see me through. As the finite security of the great *Indianapolis* slipped away beneath my feet, the infinite security of the Almighty bore me up and gave me peace—a supernatural peace promised in His Word: "Be anxious for nothing, but in everything by prayer and supplication with thanksgiving let your requests be made known to God. And the peace of God, which surpasses all comprehension, shall guard your hearts and your minds in Christ Jesus" (Philippians 4:6-7).

Abandon Ship

After almost everyone had left the quarter-deck, I stepped over the rail and walked two long steps down the side of the ship that now made a ramp into the water. I then jumped feet first into the murky, oil-laden ocean. My kapok jacket came up over my head and as I came up to the top, I desperately parted the water's surface with my hands in an effort to get my head above the layer of thick black oil. Pushing the oil away from my face, I swam away from the sinking ship about fifty yards and joined a few others who had also abandoned ship.

Together we watched in amazement as we saw the fantail going high in the air. As the ship went under, boys were frantically running up to the fantail as it gradually went vertical and then rolled to the starboard. In their panic, several quickly met their death by blindly jumping off into the four big screws that were still turning. Gradually the firelight of the steel inferno dimmed as the fantail disappeared. In the span of twelve minutes, the mighty USS *Indianapolis* slipped into her watery grave in the seven-mile depths of the Mariana Trench, the deepest region of the Pacific Ocean. There she rests to this day.

I cannot remember all that raced through my mind as I swam there in the darkness. But I do recall a powerful promise that resonated within my heart that dreadful hour, a promise that has ruled my life from that day forward. Jesus promised, "Peace I leave with you, my peace I give unto you: not as the world giveth, give I unto you. Let not your heart be troubled, neither let it be afraid" (John 14:27, KJV).

Survival is a powerful motivator. Reality sank into our minds as we watched the *Indy* sink into the sea. I looked around and began to talk with some of my young shipmates. We took inventory of our little group and discovered there were eighty of us. Since the *Indy* had continued to move ahead even after having been hit, many men had bailed off behind us and in front of us. Little groups of men were scattered over approximately one mile. At least one third of the men in my group were injured. Others were burned beyond recognition. Some men had no life jacket and hung on to their comrades who did. And to our dismay, there was not a life raft to be found. Our lives depended solely on divine providence and the kapok life vests He had supplied.

Two of my fellow Marines were in our little cluster of eighty. One had sustained such serious injury after being blown against a bulkhead that he only lasted a couple of hours. Another Marine named Spooner dove into the water headfirst, covering his face with the gooey oil. Over the next several days the oil became an excruciating irritant to his eyes. As he tried to rub the oil out of his eyes, he rubbed salt water in them. By the second day, his eyes were so inflamed that he could not shut them. His eyeballs eventually bulged out of their sockets, leaving them vulnerable to the blistering sun and salt water.

Before morning, our numbers dwindled by about one third. Most of the severely wounded were hysterical with high fevers and died during the night. When they passed on, we ceremonially removed their dog tags. We also took their life jackets and gave them to crew members who were without. We then quietly released their bodies into a watery grave. Even after releasing them, the corpses remained with us as if they were somehow still alive and afraid to leave. The gruesome sight of departed friends was a constant reminder of our potential fate and the fragility of life.

The First Day at Sea

The morning brought with it both hope and despair. We were

shivering cold and glad to feel the warmth of the rising sun. The surface water dropped to about 85 degrees at night, gradually lowering our body temperatures to dangerous levels of hypothermia. In an effort to keep us all together, our dwindling little group formed a circle by fastening our life jackets to one another. This kept us together as we were tossed to and fro by the massive crests of waves, otherwise, we could be easily separated by fifty yards in a matter of seconds.

For those of us who were able to talk, conversation naturally revolved around the topic of rescue. While no one knew for sure, we tried to assure ourselves that an S.O.S. got off the ship. Even if it hadn't, we reassured ourselves that surely the Navy would become alarmed when they discovered we failed to make our intended rendezvous the next day with the USS *Idaho*. Our hopes ebbed and flowed with the sound of every plane that flew over us, most at 30,000 feet.

The sunlight of the first day also brought with it a fear of being slaughtered by an enemy sub. Now vulnerable and easily seen, we knew that whoever torpedoed us could possibly still be around. We all surmised that we had been attacked by a Japanese sub, since we had never seen another ship. We also knew that their subs were known to surface and exterminate helpless men at sea with their machine guns. While this was a very real potential, I think most all of us had a guarded optimism that help was on its way. We told ourselves that the enemy would probably think the same thing and therefore not want to linger in the area.

As the day dragged on, we continued to lose more boys. Those who had accidentally swallowed some of the oil had been vomiting all night and were now severely dehydrated and convulsing. They gradually became delusional and would thrash the waters and shake violently until they would finally lose control of themselves. Most of these never made it through the first day.

As our bodies baked in the open sea, we began to realize that the sun was transitioning from friend to foe. It soon began to blister our previously chilled and now exposed flesh. We tore our clothing to make protective hoods to give us some shade, but the ultraviolet rays reflecting off the water still managed to find our skin. The bright light of the sun glaring off the water forced us to squint our eyes until our facial muscles became utterly exhausted. Our eyes also burned from the caustic salt-water waves that would constantly splash our face.

The 100-degree heat combined with the scorching sun brought on another enemy—thirst. Our dehydrated bodies screamed for water. What made it even more torturous is that we were literally immersed in it. Yet because of the salt, we could not drink it. Occasionally a breaking wave would catch a sailor off guard and strangle him as he fought to expel the very thing his body craved. Others foolishly tried to strain the water through their clothing, thinking such a procedure would eliminate the salt. Within a few minutes their foolishness became evident. Their tongues would begin to swell, their speech became slurred, and soon they would become hysterical. Once they reached that stage, they were beyond help and shortly perished.

Late that first day, around dusk, we had company. To our horror, we began to see large, black dorsal fins cutting through the water and circling our group. I cannot describe the fear. Yet, for some reason they seemed unwilling to launch a full attack on our little cluster. They would just circle around and around with what seemed to be a predetermination. Sadly, some of the hallucinating boys insisted on swimming away from the group to an island or ship they were sure they saw. When they did, their thrashing about would soon attract the sharks and we would hear a blood-curdling scream. Like a fishing bobber taken under the water, the helpless sailor would quickly disappear. Then his mangled body would resurface moments later with only a portion of his torso remaining. On other occasions the waves would tear one of the boys away from the group, causing him to helplessly drift into the shark-infested perimeter. Some of these were only mauled and were able to make their way back to the group. Others were not so fortunate. Over the course of the next few days, this scenario would be played out more times than I wish to recount.

The Approaching Night

Certainly our resolve to avoid drinking the water at all costs and do whatever we could to stay together was strengthened that first evening. But our hopes of rescue seemed to sink with the setting of the sun. The inexpressible fear of the sharks only worsened as the dark approached, and the thought of having to endure another shivering night was depressing. We were all miserable and helpless. As night approached, dehydrated sailors continued to become incoherent and thrashed about until all their energy was depleted.

Desperation and fear only worsened as the blackness of night enveloped our quivering bodies. The darkness seemed to isolate us in our misery, preventing us from even seeing the guy next to us. For some of the men, there was nothing to bring hope. And without hope, all that is left is despair. But for me, hope never waned. And I do not say that to my credit, but to God's. Even if the Lord chose to let me perish, I was confident knowing that His sweet providence was ultimately in charge. In fact, it was a welcomed thought to consider that He might just decide to take me to my heavenly home and relieve me from my distress. But somehow I knew that He wanted me to survive.

Had it not been for the strength and incomprehensible peace of the Lord, I fear the ordeal of the first night and day would have destroyed me. I had already seen and experienced enough human anguish and suffering to last me a lifetime. The inescapable bloody carnage alone was almost unbearable. Yet through it all, God remained my close companion. His faithful presence gave me great strength and resolve.

As the terrors of the night surrounded me, my heart ran frequently to the Lord in prayer. The indwelling Holy Spirit would help me think of Scripture. When this would happen, I would lay hold of His promises and pray them to back to Him with an attitude of awe and great joy. That night I remember quoting the 23rd Psalm, giving special emphasis to the source of my strength and hope, the Lord Himself, and to my Shepherd's personal care for me. I prayed:

"The *LORD* is *my* shepherd; *I* shall not want. *He* maketh *me* to lie down in green pastures: *he* leadeth *me* beside the still waters. *He* restoreth *my* soul: *he* leadeth *me* in the paths of righteousness for *his* name's sake. Yea, thought *I* walk through the valley of the shadow of death, *I* will fear no evil: for *Thou* art with *me; thy* rod and *thy* staff they comfort *me*. *Thou* preparest a table before *me* in the presence of mine enemies: *thou* anointest *my* head with oil; *my* cup runneth over. Surely goodness and mercy shall follow *me* all the days of *my* life: and *I* will dwell in the house of the *LORD for ever*" (Psalm 23; KJV, emphasis mine).

Sleep was intermittent during the night. Had it not been for sheer exhaustion, I probably never would have been able to even shut my eyes, much less doze off for short intervals. Yet, by God's grace, I relaxed in the darkness and rested in His care. Convinced that rescue would come in the morning, I felt encouraged and confident. Little did I know that this was only the beginning, and the worst was yet to come.

Chapter Four

Mysteries of Darkness
and Light—
the Second Day

⚓

Again therefore Jesus spoke to them, saying,
"I am the light of the world; he who follows Me
shall not walk in the darkness,
but shall have the light of life."

John 8:12

While not having been a deeply religious man, I must give credit to the power of prayer. We were five men from different parts of the United States and of different beliefs and religions. We constantly prayed to our God for rescue. I will always believe, firmly believe, the one reason that we were able to face this ordeal and, in time, to survive was the power of these prayers. Without God, we surely would have been lost.

Survivor Robert H. Brundidge

We saw sharks from day one. After a short while they became aggressive. With our legs dangling, we became easy targets. We'd hear men scream and then the water would turn red. The sharks were getting us. A shark got one of my buddies who was just a couple feet from me. The shark's tail and the water just covered me up—I was that close. If the sharks took a man's leg, or just bit him, sometimes he would float back up; some did and some didn't. Of course, they were all dead. We'd take their life jackets and their dog tags.

Survivor Loel Dene Cox

I heard someone say, "Let's say a prayer." I do not remember ever having prayed before, but I prayed silently for the first time in my life. Don't let anyone tell you he cannot pray; even an atheist cannot deny the existence of God. We prayed for our lives to be spared. We prayed to God to ease our pains. We prayed to God not to forsake us, not to let us die, to save us. We prayed for His mercy. The soothing effects of prayer linked us together as we began to try to help each other.

Survivor Buck W. Gibson

When would we be rescued? Had an SOS been sent? I relied heavily on J.J.'s opinion, "There's no doubt an SOS message was sent," J.J. said. He knew this to be true because he had sent it.

Survivor Glenn G. Morgan

My group had three floater nets and two life rafts. We tried to keep the rafts for the most severely wounded. There were approximately 200 or more in this group. Sharks swam below us, bumping our legs. I am often asked about sharks. My reply, "They don't like Irishmen!" Most of us were Christians or became Christians. We prayed daily. God was with me always.

Survivor Paul J. Murphy

I am not overly religious but I called on my Maker as earnestly as any young fellow ever did. I am sure all the others did the same. Lying there in the middle of the Pacific Ocean with nothing but water in sight reminded me of the quote, "Water, water, everywhere, but not a drop to drink."

Survivor James B. Loftis

DAWN IS ALWAYS SUCH A BEAUTIFUL SIGHT. The beginning of a new day brings with it such promise of good things to come. The sunrise of the second day was no different. It brought with it welcomed warmth for both our shivering bodies and our despondent souls. As the light dispelled the darkness, rays of hope filled my heart as I tried to convince myself that today we would be rescued. I assumed that surely by now the Navy was combing the ocean surface to find us, that any moment we would see the rescue planes hovering over us. To think otherwise would only fan the embers of desperation into a raging fire of hopelessness.

As I felt my body becoming increasingly frail, my mind would immediately take me back to that moment two nights earlier when I hung on to the ship's rail just before I abandoned ship. I would reflect upon the supernatural peace that God gave me through the unfailing promise He would bring to my mind, saying, "I will never leave you nor forsake you." Inevitably that assurance would give me strength. In fact, as I think back upon how many times the indwelling Holy Spirit brought comfort and hope to me through His written Word, I more fully appreciate the words of the psalmist when he said, "Thy word is a lamp to my feet and a light to my path" (Psalm 119:105). It was indeed God's Word that I repeated over and over throughout those days and nights, bringing me comfort, hope and confidence.

As the day began to dawn, God used the light to reveal things we did not want to see. Even before the sun began to peak over the horizon, I was gradually able to see the floating carnage of mutilated bodies all around me. And to my horror, I could see the heads of numerous sailors with whom I had spoken the evening before now face down in the water. At first I remained silent and still, paralyzed with disbelief. The eerie scene before me was like a floating battlefield on a calm sea. I tried hard to convince myself that surely some of my shipmates were just asleep. My eyes began to search through the emerging light to find life. Surely someone was awake and alive. Spooner and I had locked our legs around each other to preserve body heat through the night and avoid attracting sharks with dangling legs. But surely Spooner and I weren't the only ones left.

Soon I began to realize that during the night our entire group had drifted apart considerably. As the dawn continued to illumine the early morning, we could see and hear others beginning to stir about—a welcomed relief. During those brief minutes I experienced feelings of loneliness I hope to never feel again in this life. They caused me to be thankful for the wonderful promises of peace and eternal fellowship for those who love Christ. Heaven will be the perfect antithesis to what I experienced in that silent, lonely dawn.

Gradually the silence was broken with much conversation and chatter. Some began thrashing about in mental and physical agony. Others voiced the same concerns I was experiencing regarding men that appeared to be asleep. Slowly we began to swim toward our lifeless comrades to see if we could rouse them. For most, our efforts were futile. Because of nighttime inactivity and the eighty-five-degree water, many had succumbed to the chilling sleep of hypothermia. Historian Doug Stanton graphically describes the physiological processes of this awful phenomenon.

"At this latitude, the Pacific was a steady eighty-five degrees, warm by most ocean standards. But it was still more than ten degrees cooler than core body temperature, and since the sinking the boys had been turning hypothermic. This condition affected each survivor differently, depending on his percentage of body fat and the amount of clothing he was wearing (the more the better in terms of heat retention). But on average, the boys were losing about one degree Fahrenheit for every hour of exposure in the water during the nighttime hours, when the air temperature dropped to the mid-eighties. During the nights, which felt brutally cold in comparison to the days' nearly 100-degree heat, the boys' body temperatures dropped as much as ten degrees.

As soon as the sun set, as it did with guillotine-like speed this close to the equator, the boys started shivering uncontrollably. This was the body's way of generating heat, but it quadrupled the rate of oxygen consumed. Hypothermia depresses the central nervous system as the body slows to conserve energy, and at a core temperature of ninety-three degrees (nearly five degrees below normal), speech becomes difficult, apathy develops, and amnesia typically sets in. At around ninety-one degrees, the kidneys stop filtering the body's waste—urination stops—and hypoxia, or poisoning, commences. Breathing becomes labored, the heart beats raggedly, and consciousness dims. The afflicted fall into an inattentive stupor.

By Tuesday at dawn, Dr. Haynes estimated the core body temperatures of the *Indy*'s boys were probably hovering right around eighty-five degrees. Later, after the shark attack, as the sun rose and baked them, their temperatures began to rise a degree or two, perhaps as many as five. In essence, the boys had fallen into a pattern of abrupt energy drain and renewal. But increasingly, they were building a deficit that eventually even the heat of day wouldn't be able to erase. With their body temperatures dipping low, the boys were wobbling off into the land of fatal judgment." 1.

While hypothermia had claimed numerous victims that night, others who had sustained injuries aboard ship had also slipped into eternity after their long and constant battle swimming in the ocean, fighting the sharks and dehydration. Some of the dead had lost limbs or were disemboweled by the sharks. I'm sure they welcomed death as a merciful reprieve from their excruciating pain. There were other boys, however, who were still alive but delusional, unable to speak coherently or act rationally. Most were now too weak to scream. From them, only the sounds of faint groans could be heard. Often they could be heard pleading to God for mercy. Indeed, there are no atheists when mens' souls are suspended between life and death. I often heard sailors say, "God if You are out there, we need Your help!"

The scenes of that morning are forever etched in my mind. The inexpressible feelings of despair brought many of us to the very edge of suicide. I'm sure some of those who had passed through the veil of this life had chosen that option. Too exhausted to hold their heads up and out of the water, they simply gave up.

My Marine buddy Miles Spooner wanted to take his life. The massive amount of oil he encountered when he went into the water headfirst as he abandoned ship had caused his eyes to become two large, ulcerated sores. By now he was unable to close them and the slightest ray of light triggered enormous pain. Obviously, the sunrise was virtually unbearable, making suicide a viable alternative. He said to me, "Harrell, we know no help is coming and I can't stand this excruciating pain much longer." He repeated this several times throughout the day. I recall asking him how he would end his life, to which he replied, "I'll dive down so far that I'll drown before I come back up."

Although I knew he was miserable, I simply could not stand the thought of letting him go. So I tried to talk him out of it. Tapping deep into my own hope of survival, and my pride of being a United States Marine, I told him, "Spooner, listen to me. There are only two Marines left in this group and when everyone else is gone, I'm still going to be here and you're going to be with me. I know in my heart that God is going to deliver us and we are going to survive this together." He gave no reply. But somehow I sensed that my confidence got to him. Unsure of what he was thinking, I turned his back to me and assertively fastened his kapok jacket to mine. He seemed to relax at that point, probably more out of exhaustion than relief.

Thirst and Hallucination

As a result of the rising sun combined with the increased activity of releasing the dead from their kapok jackets, we began to warm up quickly that morning. We also seemed to be in a constant battle to round up the stragglers and care for the wounded. Quickly, however, the welcomed warmth produced yet another misery—thirst. We were desperate for water. By the time the sun reached its zenith at mid-day, our tongues were beginning to swell in our parched mouths and throats, making our speech slurred almost beyond understanding. Dehydration was becoming our new and dreaded enemy—one that had taken the place of the sharks that would come and go. The only answer for the dehydration was the one thing we did not have—fresh water. Yet we were floating in a close substitute, but one that would kill.

The wrath of mass hallucination began to plague our group with devastating results. Our group had dwindled from eighty the first day to about forty by noon the second day. Although he was not in our group, Dr. Lewis Haynes, one of the ship's doctors, later described what he saw from a medical perspective. In his book *In Harm's Way*, author Doug Stanton summarized Dr. Haynes' observations as follows:

"The dehydrated boys, their tongues swelling, their throats squeezing shut, and their minds unhinging—began drinking salt water. After hours of resisting the temptation, they drank furtively at first, as if ashamed. Then they began to gorge themselves, murmuring in pleasure as they sipped through bleeding lips from the cool mirror of the sea.

As they drank, the boys were setting off a complex series of chemical reactions, all of them volatile. The sea contains twice the salinity that the human body can safely ingest, and as the boys drank, their cells were shrinking, expanding, and exploding as they sacrificed what's called their "free water." This was the cells' attempt to lower the sodium deluging the bloodstream, and it was futile.

The boys' kidneys were scrubbing their blood before dumping it back into the circulatory system, but they were unable to keep ahead of the sodium tidal wave. Haynes knew the boys were shorting out on salt, succumbing to what in medical terms is known as hypernatremia. He watched some of them foam at the nose; a root beer-colored substance dripped down their chins as their eyes rolled back in their heads. He watched their lips turn blue, heard their breathing grow ragged. In their brains, neurons were misfiring or not firing at all. Electrical activity was disrupted in much the way a car's battery would cease to work properly if the composition of its power cells was altered. It was a continuous loop of self-destruction, and Haynes knew the only remedy was massive rehydration.

Those who succumbed fell into violent fits and, finally, comas. At first, they whooped and hollered and spun circles in the water, arms flailing, until finally a kind of explosion took place and they went limp. More than one boy came to rest in a ring of circling sharks. The dead and near-dead floated motionless, facing the sky, bodies jerking, eyes blinking in terror. Some of the poor boys clawed the air in thirst or panic. Their throats were too dry to scream. It often took no more than two hours for them to die." 2.

Dealing with hallucinating friends was extremely difficult. It was like trying to reason with an angry drunk or a disoriented Alzheimer's patient. The salt water would literally make men crazy. Occasionally a hallucinating shipmate would become violent and attack another sailor close to him. The delusional sailor would convince himself that his buddy was the enemy and go after him with a vengeance. Others would assault a shipmate, thinking he was hiding fresh water.

On several occasions I remember hallucinating sailors claiming to see a ship or an island and excitedly trying to enlist others to swim with them to safety. We tried to form a human circle in order to corral those who were the most demented. But eventually the most desperate men would break through, chasing after a mirage of oasis that didn't exist. By the second day, fatigue had set in, making it increasingly difficult to expend any energy. In our weakened condition, we were unable to fight the swells, so little by little our circle of safety deteriorated into a scattered flotilla of helpless men adrift. It was basically every man for himself. Nevertheless, we tried to reason with our irrational mates, even if it was, at times, an exercise in futility.

Inevitably, when we disagreed with them or attempted to calm them, they would become belligerent and often vicious. Invectives would spew forth from confused and angry hearts. I would try to apply Scripture when I spoke to them, remembering that "A gentle answer turns away wrath, but a harsh word stirs up anger" (Proverbs 15:1). Kindness and agreement would occasionally calm them down, but only temporarily. It was exhausting to try and prevent them from hysterically swimming away from the group. Those who left the safety of the group would soon begin to flail about in the waters, struggling with fatigue and insanity. This, of course, would draw the attention of the sharks. Soon we would hear a bloodcurdling scream of terror and watch the helpless victim disappear, then surface again with his remains being fought over by other sharks; a haunting sound and scene I cannot erase from my mind.

I vividly remember an incident on that day with a sixteen-year-old sailor who had been aboard ship less than three weeks. He lied about his age in order to join the Navy (along with his twin brother who was also on board but not in our group). Dehydration had taken its toll on him. The illusions of hallucination had seized his mind. Like others before him, he began to get increasingly excited, flailing and splashing about, looking around with a nervous enthusiasm. Seeing me, he swam over and insisted that the "scuttlebutt was open!"—Navy talk for access to a drinking fountain aboard ship. Frantically he stuck his face into the water and pointed down at his fantasy. No reasoning to the contrary would dissuade him. He was utterly convinced of his salvation. Screaming hysterically with jubilation, he removed his life vest and all his clothes. Because he had not been aboard ship long enough to get a suntan, his body was lily white. I can still see him slowly disappear into the depths of the Pacific as he swam after a figment of his imagination.

As the day wore on, hope continued to wane for all of us. A man can endure just about anything as long as he has hope. But take away his hope, and all that is left is despair and the relief of suicide. We frequently saw planes flying overhead, but they were flying at 30,000 feet. Many of them were our B-29 bombers on bombing missions in Japan. Gradually we just tuned them out and ignored them. The relentless cycle of hope followed by despair was simply too painful to endure.

Prayer Meeting at Sea

Although my understanding of spiritual issues was immature and my faith largely untested as a young man, I nevertheless possessed an unwavering assurance that I would be saved, both physically and spiritually. Although I did not fully understand it at the time, my confidence emanated from the Holy Spirit of God living within me, and every person united to Christ through faith. I now realize that my confident hope was not something manufactured in my will, but rather, as the apostle Paul reminds us, "The Spirit Himself bears witness with our spirit that we are children of

God, and if children, heirs also, heirs of God and fellow heirs with Christ, if indeed we suffer with Him, in order that we may also be glorified with Him" (Romans 8:16-17). I also tenaciously hung on to the comforting promise that gripped my heart when I first abandoned ship: "Peace I leave with you, my peace I give unto you: not as the world giveth, give I unto you. Let not your heart be troubled, neither let it be afraid" (John 14:27, KJV).

As the years have come and gone, that same confident hope that sustained me in the sea has grown in substance and in subjective awareness—the very hope exalted by the inspired apostle Peter. Knowing he was about to be crucified for the cause of Christ, Peter encouraged the first century Christians as they persevered under enormous persecution, comforting them saying:

"Blessed be the God and Father of our Lord Jesus Christ, who according to His great mercy has caused us to be born again to a *living hope* through the resurrection of Jesus Christ from the dead, to obtain an inheritance which is imperishable and undefiled and will not fade away, reserved in heaven for you, who are protected by the power of God through faith for a salvation ready to be revealed in the last time. In this you *greatly rejoice*, even though now for a little while, if necessary, you have been distressed by various trials, that the proof of your faith, being more precious than gold which is perishable, even though tested by fire, may be found to result in praise and glory and honor at the revelation of Jesus Christ; and though you have not seen Him, you love Him, and though you do not see Him now, but believe in Him, you *greatly rejoice with joy inexpressible and full of glory*, obtaining as the outcome of your faith the salvation of your souls" (1 Peter 1:3-9; emphasis mine).

Only God knows how many other men shared my faith and experienced the same spiritual assurance. Certainly many, if not most of the men prayed. Their prayers would sound something like this: "God, if you're out there somewhere, we need your help. I don't want to die. None of us want to die. I have a family back home. Please save us!" Seldom would they close with an "amen" because the unbearable pathos of their heart would overflow into uncontrollable sobbing. The vividness of these memories haunts me to this day—a source of perpetual grief.

As the day wore on, I continued to pray and quote portions of Scripture that came to mind. They brought comfort to my aching heart, even as God has promised, "The steadfast of mind Thou wilt keep in perfect peace, because he trusts in Thee" (Isaiah 26:3). Years later my Marine buddy Miles Spooner gave an interview to a newspaper where the reporter described Spooner's reflections of me saying, "Harrell, a 'hard-shell' Christian, (who) quoted Bible verses, prayed, and pleaded with God during their extended time afloat. 'I didn't care much for religion then,' Spooner said, but he's changed his mind over the years. Did religion save him and Harrell? 'Probably so,' he said, in a choked voice." I am thankful that the Lord gave me a steadfast hope and a spiritual desire to commune with Him during such an agonizing ordeal. Make no mistake; it was the God of the Bible, not mere religion, that saved us.

Answered Prayer in a Cloud

The monotony of the waves was mesmerizing. Over and over again, the lumbering swells hoisted us high into the air and then gently lowered us into the infinite valleys of the Pacific. But we continued to pray. After many hours of persistent supplication, a possible answer seemed to appear in the distance. It was a small dark cloud—a harbinger of life-giving water. I can still visualize that little cloud drawing closer and closer. Eventually we could see the rain falling from it. Our hearts pounded within us as we begged God to steer it in over our gaping mouths. With swollen tongues we cried out to God for just a few drops of the life sustaining fluid. Within a matter of minutes, our prayers were answered. The fresh, cool water beat hard against our sunburned faces. We used our hands to funnel as much water as we could into our parched mouths. I remember weeping with joy as I opened my mouth heavenward and drank freely from His kind provision.

That incident always reminds me of the object lesson Jesus used with a Samaritan women who came to draw water from a well. Contrasting our need for water to sustain us physically with the greater need of spiritual transformation, He said, "Everyone who drinks of this water shall thirst again; but whoever drinks of the water that I shall give him shall never thirst; but the water that I shall give him shall become in him a well of water springing up to eternal life" (John 4:13b-14). How true. That rain cloud over the Pacific only provided temporary relief for my body. But the miracle of my new birth in Christ has satisfied my soul from the day I confessed Him as Savior and Lord to this very day. I have drunk from the well of His mercy and grace every day of my life, and the reservoir of His faithfulness and grace has never run dry.

Black Dorsal Fins

When the brief rain shower was over, the sun once again glared down upon our sunburnt bodies. Our eyelids were severely swollen and the moisture on our lips quickly dissipated in the hot sun, leaving them exposed, cracked and bleeding. The membranes of our eyes and noses were also highly irritated. Most of the boys were nearly blind. I cut the sleeves out of my dungaree jacket and spread them over my face, not only for protection from the sun, but also to prevent the dangerous salt water from splashing into my nose and mouth and strangling me. I knew I had to avoid drinking the dangerous brine at all cost. So I constantly fought the turbulent waves to avoid being strangled. Occasionally the poisonous saline would catch me a bit off guard and I would end up with a mouth full. I would immediately begin to gag for my very life—a task that required me to expend precious energy.

Desperate for water, some boys would tear off a piece of clothing and use it to strain salt out of the water—or so they thought. They would hold it over their mouth and have a buddy cup his hands and pour water over the cloth, foolishly thinking they were extracting at least some of the salt. Soon they too would become prey for the sharks that were always lingering close by. Those who were married with families fought harder to avoid the temptation to drink. Many later admitted that visions of their wives and family kept them alive. But many others had nothing to restrain them from risking their lives with such a silly experiment.

The scene around me on that second day can only be likened to a nightmare. Human remains and corpses floated all around our dwindling group. The sharks were never far away, lingering in the distance, occasionally picking off a straggler. Often they would suddenly swim toward us for no apparent reason. Those of us who could still see remember with horror those black dorsal fins slicing through the water. When they would swim through our ranks, hysteria would naturally overwhelm us. It was probably even worse for those nearly blind who could hear the terrifying screams, but were unable to clearly see the ferocious predator. On numerous occasions I recall seeing a large fin coming straight at me. In horror I would take what I thought would be my last breath, bend my knees up to my chest, draw up my feet to my buttocks and cry out to God, "Oh God help!" Sometimes I could feel a fin brush my body. Other times I would merely feel the wake of the massive beast streaking through the water just underneath me. These gut-wrenching encounters caused me to feel as though I was constantly tied up in a knot.

Excruciating body cramps would often follow these episodes. Every muscle fiber in my body would tense up to make me as small a target as I could possibly become. When the sharks would become active, my weakened body would finally get to a point where I could no longer draw my knees up to my chest. My abdominal muscles would become completely exhausted, leaving my legs to helplessly dangle in the path of the mighty marauders. Although by God's providence I was spared from the sharks, the trauma of those encounters over four and one-half days at sea later manifested itself in what was diagnosed as the most severe case of pelvic lipomatosis the doctors had ever seen. They believed that the prolonged exposure to cold water, combined with the torturous stress of extreme panic, had ultimately caused a lipoma (a benign tumor of fat tissues) to form in and around my colon, bladder and stomach cavity, resulting in major surgery years later.

The winds and the sea began to pick up later that afternoon and evening. We were steadily losing a sailor every few hours. Our weakened bodies were no match for the powerful ocean. We would have given anything for even a raft. Unable to swim and stay together, our shrinking little group was systematically dispersed over several hundred yards as night began to fall.

By now our kapok jackets were beginning to lose their buoyancy. They were not designed to keep a man afloat for more than forty-eight hours, and we were now beyond that limit. As they became increasingly water-logged, our bodies naturally rode deeper in the water, putting us at even greater risk of strangulation and drowning. Making it worse, the rough canvas on what was commonly referred to as "the horse collar," had become an irritant to our necks, chins and any other body part where it was free to rub. These rubs became raw and infected sores due to the salt water and oil. Salt-water ulcers, as they were called, were also being added to the list of tortures. Open wounds began to develop in every fold of skin on our bodies. Those at the bend of the arm, the armpit and behind the knees were the worst for me. Later these wounds would prove to be my greatest external physical injury, requiring me to be wrapped with Vaseline gauze for days in the base hospital on Guam.

Some of the boys wore rubber life belts instead of kapok jackets. However, they soon discovered that most of them leaked. Often the sailors would wear them (not inflated) around their waste aboard ship during combat as a precaution in case they had to suddenly abandon ship. If that happened, they could then inflate the belt and hopefully remain afloat until they were rescued.

Unfortunately, the prolonged exposure to sunlight aboard ship caused the rubber to dry rot and crack, greatly reducing their ability to retain air for any sustained period of time. Worse yet, a rubber belt around the waist has a tendency to throw the body into a prone position rather than holding it erect. The poor boys that wore them were always fighting to stay upright.

As darkness approached and the seas churned, hope of rescue continued to wane. By the end of the second day, our group had dwindled to around thirty. And now we faced another shivering night, lost at sea.

Chapter Five

From Light to Starless Night— the Third Day

⚓

Who gives the sun for light by day,

And the fixed order of the moon and the stars

for light by night,

Who stirs up the sea so that its waves roar;

The LORD of hosts is His name.

Jeremiah 31:35

I thought we would be picked up the next morning. After all, we were the flagship of the Fifth Fleet. Night came! Then another night! The third day was terrible with sharks under and all around us. Everyone was starting to get delirious. The fourth day was chaos! From hundreds of men . . . we were now down to small groups.

Survivor Lloyd P. Barto

On the third or fourth day, our life jackets became saturated. More men were lost. We had to turn their life lines loose, as they would have pulled us down. More and more men turned to prayer. Several sang the "Navy Hymn" which we had sung every Sunday morning aboard ship. . ."for those in peril on the sea."

Survivor William R. Mulvey

On the morning of the third day, I was shocked to see the condition of the other guys around me. They were hallucinating from being so dehydrated. We were hungry and thirsty. On our bodies we had huge sores that made us miserable. I remember a fellow survivor who floated up to me and told me to look at the tag on my kapok life jacket. I looked down and saw that it read "Good for 48 hours." Some men started to drift away from the group, telling us they were going to an island or a ship or to land that they saw just ahead. I remember one guy who started taking off his life jacket and telling me that the ship was just below the surface and that we could go to the water fountain. I tried to restrain him, but he just slipped away and never came back. By now, over half of the original group was gone. I was floating in the most horrible sea you could imagine. There was blood and oil mixed with parts of bodies and half-eaten corpses still floating in their life jackets. And I was only eighteen years old!

Survivor Harold A. Eck

I met a friend that had a rubber belt like mine. We stuck together, telling each other that we would make it and not to give up. We took turns, one sleeping while the other made sure he stayed awake. After three or four days, he looked at me and said, "I can't take this anymore." We started to pray, and that is when he gave me his life belt . . . then he went down. I tried, but I could not reach him. I gave his belt to another, hoping he would make it. I have tried to remember his name but just can't. I know with the good Lord's help, I will see him again.

Survivor Lindsey L. Carter

By this time I would have given my front seat in heaven and walked the rotten log all the way through hell for just one cool drink of water. My mouth was so dry it was like cotton. How I got up enough nerve to take a mouth full of salt water, rinse my mouth, and spit it out I don't know, but I did. Did it a couple of times before the morning was over. That's probably why I ended up with saltwater ulcers in my throat. When we got picked up my throat was bigger than my head.

Survivor Woodie E. James

H YPOTHERMIA INCREASED ITS GRIP as the hours passed during the second full night. As if floating in an immense dungeon filled with cool water, I found myself constantly fighting to remain sane. The chilling numbness of body and soul would cause me to drift in and out of reality. At times it was hard to know if I was dreaming, or if I was indeed hopelessly adrift in the deepest part of the Pacific Ocean. But the sounds of the night had a way of quickly jarring me back to reality.

Off and on, all through the night, I could hear dying sailors thrashing around in the water as their bodies gradually succumbed to the insanity of salt water poisoning. The crazy, incoherent jabber describing some hallucination in their mind was always a certain indication that they would soon be gone. Every hour there seemed to be at least one or two that were out of control, swimming around with no idea where they were going. It was futile to try and help them. They seemed to have superhuman strength in the final, frenzied minutes of their life, making it dangerous to get near them for fear that they would pull us under with them. We all knew that it was best to merely stay away from them and conserve what little energy we had left.

The sharks remained with us that second night. Though we could not see them, we occasionally felt their wake, and at times, their actual body. This, of course, would trigger horrific screams of panic. It was bedlam—a nightmare of death and dying. Needless to say, it was almost impossible to sleep, though our bodies were exhausted. Spooner and I continued to fasten our kapok jackets together and lock our legs together for stability and warmth. Occasionally, when things would die down for a few minutes, we would doze off briefly and relax, only to be reawakened by more screams and thrashing.

Eventually the darkness of night gave way to dawn. Once again, the sun was a welcomed relief to our shivering bodies. It was hard to imagine that we were now beginning our third day at sea. My mind would vacillate between hope and despair. Sometimes I would think positively, assuring myself that a search and rescue operation was combing the ocean for us and would soon find us. I would think of my family and friends back home, and smile as I thought about my girlfriend in Murray, Kentucky. I would convince myself that we would all soon be reunited. Then my hopes would give way to reality as my weakening condition and the floating carnage all around me gave irrefutable evidence that I could not hang on much longer. Yet, in the midst of my inner anguish, the Holy Spirit of God would always have the final say. In ways I cannot explain, He would bring a supernatural peace and assurance to my desperate soul. God was ever so faithful to His promise found in Philippians 4:6-7, "Be anxious for nothing, but in everything by prayer and supplication with thanksgiving let your requests be made known to God. And the peace of God, which surpasses all comprehension, shall guard your hearts and your minds in Christ Jesus."

The morning light of the third day revealed that our numbers had now dwindled to only seventeen—a mere fraction of the original eighty in my group. As usual, the seas were rough, tossing us around like rubber balls. Back and forth we rocked in a torturous rhythm that only added to our fatigue. As the sun grew brighter and began to bear down upon us, our parched throats and tongues swelled so badly that we could hardly talk.

While we were thankful to be alive, we all were in need of encouragement and hope. So we began to pray once again. From about 10:00 A.M. to 1:00 P.M. each man poured his heart out to their Maker, begging Him for physical deliverance and promising spiritual reformation in return. Mingled with our prayers were passionate conversations describing our families and friends back home. Some of the men were almost gone, unable to even speak. Others were in varying stages of hallucination due to salt water poisoning. But those who could, prayed.

Clearly there were no atheists in the water that day. Gone was that damnable attitude of pride that deceives men into thinking that there is no God, or if there is, they don't need Him. When a man is confronted with death, it is the face of Almighty God he sees, not his own. We were all acutely aware of our Creator during those days and nights. Our little seventeen-member prayer meeting attested to this. Every man knew he was dying. It was only a matter of hours. Only a miracle could save us. So we prayed for a miracle. Men prayed like I have never heard men pray. With inconsolable grief each man poured out his heart to God. With swollen tongues we did our best taking turns pleading with God for deliverance. But before one could finish, another would interrupt with *his* supplications. Another would then speak of his wife and children, and then cry out to God to be reunited with them. Because of dehydration, there were very few tears rolling down our grimacing faces. It was as though the ocean now contained them all. On that third morning and early afternoon, seventeen dying men begged God for mercy with a cacophony of sobs and groans the likes of which I have never experienced since that day.

The Makeshift Raft

The prayer meeting was emotionally exhausting. As things got quiet among us, we once again surrendered to the sea in an almost catatonic stupor. Silently we floated, back and forth. Up and down. Curious sharks would periodically make their way through our ranks, slowly and deliberately, only to disappear without incident. While I have no way of knowing the minds of my comrades, certainly for me there still remained a glimmer of hope hidden away in some secret recess of my heart. The indwelling Spirit of God, my resident Comforter, continued to give me the perfect measure of grace to bear up under the weight of despair. Such is His promise found in Romans 15:13 where we are told that "the God of hope fill you with all joy and peace in believing, that you may abound in hope by the power of the Holy Spirit." Likewise we are told to "come boldly unto the throne of grace, that we may obtain mercy, and find grace to help in time of need" (Hebrews 4:16, KJV)—an admonition I frequently obeyed.

Within minutes after our prayer time concluded, around 1:00 P.M. (I still have the watch I wore and it still works), we ascended a large swell and to our amazement, we could see in the distance what appeared to be a makeshift raft surrounded by a few men. We thought that there were others out there somewhere, but we had no way of knowing for sure. We could faintly hear some chatter and knew that it had to be some of ours. After making contact, both little groups gradually made their way toward a central rendezvous. As we got closer to them, I could see that there was no one on the raft, but there were five sailors swimming and pulling the little raft ever so slowly in our direction. We were elated to know that at least there were a few others that had survived.

After exchanging some very warm greetings, we learned that

they were trying to swim to the Philippines, thinking that if they could get a little closer to the islands they would be more likely to be spotted. As they came alongside our group we observed that the raft consisted of two 40 mm ammunition cans and four wood slatted potato or orange crates all lashed together with strips of cloth. When I observed what was on the little raft, I saw a real answer to our prayers. To my surprise there were several kapok life jackets tied on the top. We soon discovered that they had been removed from deceased boys and had been placed atop the little flotilla to dry out. This meant that these could be used for spare jackets when ours played out—an immediate concern. While no one could possibly get on the raft, it was a welcomed sight, and I accepted it again as God answering our prayers.

The sailors with the raft were quite adamant that no one was looking for us otherwise we would already have been rescued. Although none of us wanted to admit it, down deep we all agreed. In light of this stark reality, they had decided to swim toward the Philippines—500 miles to the west, though we didn't know it. Their logic was simple: the closer we get to the Philippines, the greater our chance of being spotted and rescued.

After explaining their plans, they asked if any of us wanted to join them. Seeing the kapok jackets drying in the sun on the raft, and not having a better idea, I immediately said to my marine buddy Spooner, "I'm going to join them." He responded, "If you go Harrell, I'm going with you." So we left our little group; two

Marines joining five sailors, heading for the Philippines. We said our farewells to the fifteen sailors we had been with, each convinced we would never survive such a foolhardy venture. To my knowledge, that is the last I ever saw of them to this day.

With a renewed sense of direction and welcomed buoyancy, we grabbed hold of the strings and pieces of cloth that lashed our little flotilla together and set a course for the Philippines. Ever so gently we cupped our hands and stroked the water while our fatigued legs did their best to kick. I'm sure that most of our progress was only in our minds, but at least it gave us some sense of taking charge of our situation. Refusing to admit the magnitude of the task before us, we stroked and kicked, making headway for a time. However, our weakened bodies soon proved to be no match for the force of the ocean. Nevertheless, we forged ahead with a determined spirit, and were soon out of sight of our shipmates.

Divine Provision

As the sun was sinking in the West, about three or four hours after we had joined our Philippine-bound comrades, we noticed something on the water about 200 yards forward and off to the starboard at about 100 yards. At first we were in hopes that it was one of our shipmates. It looked as though it may have been one of our boys. But as favorable swells helped us get closer, we began to make out what appeared to be floating debris or perhaps a partially submerged crate bobbing on the surface. Curious to know what it was and what might possibly be inside, I insisted on swimming out to investigate. I really felt compelled to go, even though it meant spending reserved energy. Not seeing any sharks for several hours, I insisted on checking it out, hoping to find food.

As I slowly made my way to the strange debris, I remember praying something like, "Lord, please let there be food in this crate. Please provide. You alone are our hope." As I got closer, it became obvious that indeed it was a wooden crate. The top was partly open and I could see that there were potatoes floating inside. I thanked the Lord for His provision while frantically reaching for the potatoes. As I grabbed hold of the first potato, my heart nearly stopped beating as I realized it was rotten. But as I squeezed it in torment I found that it was solid on the inside. The rot oozed through my fingers as I compressed the precious spud until my palm felt the hard inner core, which I quickly popped in my mouth. I then grabbed another, using my teeth to hurriedly peel away the putrefying outer layer, then devoured it as well. To my delight the crate was half full of potatoes—rotten on the outside, but to a starving young man, delicious on the inside. Once again the Lord had come to our rescue. The day before He provided water; now He provided food.

With great rejoicing I praised the Lord for His provision. My prayer had been answered, giving me a renewed confidence that He would answer my greater prayer of ultimate rescue. After eating only three or four of the half-rotten potatoes, I felt that I was full, so I began stuffing all the potatoes I could in the pockets of my dungarees. Then I grabbed the crate and began to swim back to my buddies. With the smile of a conquering general I made my way back to my shipmates. As I got within earshot of them, they began hollering, "What is it? What took you so long?" I hollered back, "Potatoes—half-rotten potatoes!" I'll never forget the joy on their faces when we all gathered around that little wooden dinner table.

There had been few opportunities to truly be happy since we entered the water. But the Lord changed all that with those potatoes—at least for a short while. Although our physical condition would not allow us to eat much, we ate enough to give us at least a little nourishment and a whole lot of encouragement.

Nightfall—the Third Full Night

With renewed zeal fueled by a few morsels of food and perhaps a tablespoon of water, we entered into our third full night. It was now Wednesday evening, some sixty-six hours since we first entered the water at midnight on Sunday. As the sun began to set, we noticed the skies were becoming overcast. While the darkness of night gave relief from the burning sun, it was always a foreboding prospect. Darkness naturally casts a spell upon man, even in the best of times. But darkness at sea is especially ominous. It produces a special kind of terror, even more so on an overcast night where the clouds obscure the hope-giving luminaries of the moon and stars. Without light, you are unable to see anything, including the horizon. The blackness of the night wraps itself around you with an infinite darkness causing a surreal disorientation and profound isolation. This, combined with the menacing sharks, produced a level of fear that was numbing. It was as if we were corpses suspended somewhere between life and death. Naturally, without the moon and stars, we had no compass. And without a view of the Southern Cross, we had no way to determine our bearing and continuing our imaginary progress toward the Philippines. As the canopy of darkness gradually fell upon us, we had no choice but to merely hang on to the raft and let the great ocean take us where it would.

As I ponder that night, I often find my mind going to the inspired psalmist where he describes the Almighty as the One "who made the heavens with skill . . . who spread out the earth above the waters . . . who made the great lights . . . The sun to rule by day . . . the moon and stars to rule by night, For His lovingkindness is everlasting" (Psalm 136:5-9). Indeed, those brilliant stars shouted the glory of God on those lonesome nights. It is fascinating to think that "He counts the number of the stars; He gives names to all of them" (Psalm 147:4). Since that dreary night, I never take for granted the ineffable glory and majesty of God displayed in the luminaries He created. Again, the psalmist perfectly summarizes my thoughts when he says, "When I consider Thy heavens, the work of Thy fingers, the moon and the stars, which Thou hast ordained; What is man, that Thou dost take thought of him? And the son of man, that Thou dost care for him?" (Psalm 8:3-4). I also reflect upon the prophet Jeremiah's words when he exalted the LORD of hosts saying, "Who gives the sun for light by day, and the fixed order of the moon and the stars for light by night, who stirs up the sea so that its waves roar; The LORD of hosts is His name" (Jeremiah 31:35).

Voices Piercing the Darkness

I don't recall much of what happened as the night wore on, not until around midnight when the sound of voices suddenly pierced the darkness. We knew it must be some of our shipmates, so we began to yell out to them triggering an immediate response.

Gradually they made their way over to our little flotilla. Because of the darkness, I'm not sure to this day how many there were. They came straggling in one or two at a time. I think there may have been five or six. We were all drifting around the raft for some time, talking and not really knowing what to do. They too were proposing to swim closer to the Philippines in hopes of being spotted.

There was one naval officer in the group that I immediately recognized. He was Lt. McKissick. I had stood watch on the bridge for the captain when he was the officer of the deck. I had learned to really appreciate him aboard ship. He was from Texas and a peach of a guy. He made it easier for me to relay messages to the captain and would often repeat them to me to make sure that I had them right before he sent me off.

After a few minutes of conversation, it was obvious that Lt. McKissick was the officer in charge. He deserved that not only because of rank, but also because of his winsome character. Men automatically respected him. I couldn't hold back the fact that I still had a pocket full of half-rotten potatoes, so I shared them with our reunited shipmates. As one might well imagine, they gladly ate them, half-rotten though they were.

Together both groups discussed plans to press on toward the Philippines. At first, Lt. McKissick seemed a bit reticent to proceed ahead encumbered by the raft. Yet the prospect of extra life jackets was also a fact worthy of serious consideration. So we agreed to push on, raft and all. What happened after that is lost forever in my memory. Somewhere in the early hours of that fourth morning while it was still black as pitch, I became separated from the raft and most of my shipmates, including my Marine buddy Spooner. The next thing I remember occurred on the morning of the fourth day.

My kapok jacket had become so water-logged that it would no longer keep my head above water. I had obviously taken it off, turned it upside-down, and now I was sitting on it. I remember having to constantly paddle with my hands to hold myself erect, otherwise the jacket had just enough buoyancy to flip me over, which it did on numerous occasions. I also recall looking frantically for Spooner, but he was nowhere to be found. I was too weak to yell, and believed it wouldn't do any good anyway. I was convinced he had perished, and battled the possibility that I soon would do the same. Apart from the unfailing presence of my Lord, I had only two companions with me that morning—one sailor, whose head was already face down in the water, and Lt. McKissick.

I became increasingly confused that morning. On the one hand, I remained convinced that somehow God would rescue me. But on the other hand, I knew that I had been lost at sea for four days. My original group of eighty had now diminished to only one other man. All I could see around me was human carnage. I could literally taste the stench of rotting flesh floating here and there on the surface. Curious sharks continued to appear and disappear. From time to time I could see their fins slicing through the water and occasionally watch them pass beneath me. By this time, I was too exhausted be afraid. It was during the early morning hours of the fourth day that reality caused me to reevaluate my perspective. My hope of surviving was waning and I began to entertain the possibility that the Lord was going to rescue me in a different way. I started thinking that perhaps He would deliver me not only from the sea, but from life on earth altogether. Yet somehow the will to survive would not let me give up.

What happened next can only be described as an amazing display of divine sovereignty—an unbelievable series of events that not only saved my physical life, but also set into motion the rescue of many souls since then who have, because of this testimony, also placed their trust in the Savior.

Chapter Six

Ducks on the Pond—
the Fourth Day

⚓

Since I am afflicted and needy,
Let the Lord be mindful of me;
Thou art my help and my deliverer;
Do not delay, O my God.

Psalm 40:17

My greatest jubilation came after dark. We were looking toward the sky and could see a great beam of light that appeared to come down from heaven. I for one am convinced it came from God, although it came to us from the first ship to arrive on the scene. This happened to be the ship that picked me up out of danger after one hundred and eight hours. My rescue ship was the USS Cecil J Doyle, *and I am forever grateful to the men of that great ship.*

Survivor William R. Akines

On the fourth day, a boy from Oklahoma saw the sharks eat his best friend. I suppose that was more than his brain could stand. He took his knife which was about twelve inches long, placed it in his mouth (like Tarzan did in the movies), and started chasing sharks. They would stay just far enough ahead of him that he couldn't touch them. He would go under for long periods at a time, making us wonder whether he would come up. I don't know how long this went on, but sooner or later, I noticed that he wasn't around. Every day there seemed to be more people drinking the salt water. Also, more being eaten by sharks.

Survivor Sherman C. Booth

We lost a lot of good young men the first three days in the water. I think it was on the fourth day that I was hanging on the side of the net and this sailor came floating by—his mouth and tongue were just full of salt water sores. I grabbed him and tied him as best I could to the net, but he got away during the night.

Survivor Harold J. Bray Jr.

At the time another raft was dropped, and I started to swim after it. Soon I found out I was out of gas and I just quit swimming. It was at that moment that I heard the voice scream at me, "Grab the ring, grab the ring." I found the life ring in front of me, and I grabbed it. I was pulled aboard Captain Adrian Marks' PBY and I was a SURVIVOR!

Survivor Edward J. Brown

On the morning of the fourth day, there were even fewer of us. I counted forty people and four rafts. Then I decided that most of the forty were out of their minds. I rounded up ten who seemed to be sane enough and we took one raft and separated from the rest. It was getting too difficult to sort out the hallucinations and the real world. . . It was a raw case of survival of the fittest.

Survivor Donald J. Blum

M Y MEMORIES ARE LIMITED as I reflect upon the fourth morning. But I do recall being precariously seated in and on top of my water-logged kapok jacket. By now, mental and physical exhaustion had become harbingers of death. I was so weak that I could barely move my arms and hands to help me stay seated. My mental attitude was besieged with thoughts of surrendering to the sea. I am certain that the Lord's all-seeing eye remained fixed upon me as my impoverished body bobbed atop the massive ocean. In light of this, I often think of the psalmist's testimony of God's omnipresence and intimate care of His own found in Psalm 139:9b-10a where we read, "If I dwell in the remotest part of the sea, even there Thy hand will lead me, and Thy right hand will lay hold of me." Certainly the ministering spirits of His angelic host were actively engaged in my survival, for by now, I was almost gone. While I could not see them, I am sure they protected me as promised: "He will give His angels charge concerning you, to guard you in all your ways. They will bear you up in their hands, lest you strike your foot against a stone" (Psalm 91:11-12).

As I would think of giving up, my mind would suddenly transcend my desperate state and become fixated on thoughts of my mom and dad, six brothers and two sisters and my girlfriend waiting for me in the beautiful rolling hills of western Kentucky. Immediately such thoughts would invigorate me to push on. With renewed determination I would tell myself, "I can't give up now. Lord, help me not to give up!"

It was hard to look at the dead sailor drifting along with us—a man I never even knew. It was as though I was looking at myself in a few hours. I couldn't bear to allow my mind to think about him and the family that would mourn him. Instead, I forced myself to look only at the living. McKissick was now my only live companion. Unable to see or hear anyone else, I assumed we were the last to still be alive. Although I beat myself up at times for leaving the raft to follow him, I would always end up convincing myself that I did the right thing. After all, I needed to follow someone. And I was certainly in no condition to lead. Besides, McKissick had promised to take me to the Philippines!

For reasons I cannot explain, I remember referring to him as "Uncle Edwin"—one of my dad's brothers and a close friend back in Kentucky. I suppose my borderline delirious condition, combined with wishful thinking, caused me to project upon McKissick the image of someone safe, strong and part of the family I longed to see. Together, we struggled to stay together that fourth morning. This was a formidable task given the ten to twelve foot swells that gently lifted us high, only to lower us once again into the depths of the saline valleys. By early afternoon, the hypnotic rhythm of the waves only added to my body's craving for sleep. On several occasions I remember dozing off momentarily, only to be awakened by the frightening reality of tumbling off my life-saving seat.

On one such occasion, later on that fourth morning, I remember being aroused from one of those thirty-second catnaps by something far more terrifying. Suddenly, something hit me and splashed water all around me. I was knocked off my little perch and sent flailing into the water. My instant reaction was that another shark had bumped me. I tried frantically to get my life jacket back down under me before he could return. Desperately my exhausted muscles fought the water until I got back into the only secure position available to me—as laughable as that may seem.

When I finally got seated again, I looked, and to my astonishment a million little fish swarmed all around me. These little creatures, about twelve inches long, were everywhere. They were constantly nudging me as they darted back and forth. Evidently I was a curiosity to them, and they certainly were a welcomed sight to me. They were a pleasant relief from the sharks I had anticipated! Furiously I tried to catch them with my hands, but to no avail. Whenever I moved, they would all move, as if they were one giant organism. Somehow that little encounter brought much needed encouragement to me. I suppose it distracted me a bit, causing me to focus on life rather than death.

The First Plane

No sooner had my depleted supply of adrenalin died down from the little fish incident, than suddenly it shot back up again in an exhilarating rush. I heard a plane. Not one flying at 30,000 feet. This one was much lower. My eyes scanned the horizon to spot it. The sound seemed to be coming from every direction, making visual contact difficult. My heart pounded inside my chest. I yelled over at McKissick, "I hear a plane!" He yelled back, "So do I!" I thought to myself, could this be what we have been waiting for? Were our prayers soon to be answered? Suddenly we spotted it. And yes, it was much lower than expected. And it was flying on a course directly over us.

Oblivious to our fatigue, we began screaming around our enlarged tongues. Splashing, waving, praying, "Oh God, please let it be! Please let him see us!" My mind raced with thoughts of, "Would he see us? Could he see us?" As the plane got within about one quarter of a mile, it suddenly took a dive and came right at us within a few hundred feet. We had been spotted! We knew it! The plane then circled over us a couple of times at a very low altitude, then climbed back up and circled us a few times. We noticed the plane had wheels on it, making it impossible to land on the water. But we were confident the pilot would radio for help. Suddenly he dove back down and circled us at a much slower speed. Then he severely banked the plane and dropped us a life raft. He then tilted his wings a couple of times as if to say, "Hang on! We see you!" Then he rose up above us and continued circling.

McKissick began to slowly make his way to the raft that had been dropped within 100 yards or so from him. In order to swim, I had to once again put on my water-logged jacket upon which I had been sitting, and fight the swells and the wind that had picked up significantly. The wind also kept blowing the raft away from us. As I fought my way to the raft, I remember passing by the deceased sailor that had floated along with us all day. I paused momentarily to say a final farewell. Within a couple of hours after I reached the raft, another plane arrived on the scene. To my great relief, this one was a PBY, capable of landing on water. Help was finally on the way.

Only the marvelous providence of God can account for what had just happened. Later we learned that Lieutenant Chuck Gwinn was the pilot that dropped us the life raft and hovered over us until help could come on that eventful afternoon. His plane was a Lockheed Ventura PV-1 bomber used to search and destroy Japanese submarines. As Gwinn patrolled the waters at about 3,000 feet, a recurring problem with a weighted antenna sock set our unexpected sighting in motion. This sock was used to prevent the long whip antenna from flailing about. Evidently the troublesome sock had come off, causing the antenna to whip back and forth against the side of the plane—a potentially dangerous situation. Gwinn decided to leave the cockpit and assist his bombardier, Joe Johnson, in coming up with some kind of remedy for the problem. As he looked out the bomb bay window in the floor of the airplane to consider a creative solution, his ever vigilant and well-trained eyes unexpectedly fell upon some minute shining objects on the water below. As he looked more closely, he noticed what he thought was some kind of discoloration on the water. He hurriedly climbed back into the cockpit and dropped down for a closer look, thinking perhaps it was an oil slick from a wounded enemy submarine.

By the time he reached about three hundred feet, to their amazement, the crew began to detect the oil soaked heads of many men scattered in twos and threes, their heads bobbing on the water. In fact, the water was filled with debris, corpses and empty kapok life jackets mingled among many sharks. Then they spotted about thirty greasy survivors splashing and waving—fellow survivors McKissick and I were unable to see. Some were swimming alone, others clinging to life rafts. Realizing the unknown survivors were in immediate danger, Chuck Gwinn broke radio silence declaring, "Ducks on the pond!" 1. He then immediately radioed headquarters on Peleliu and reported, SIGHTED 30 SURVIVORS 011-30 NORTH 133-30 EAST. 2.

Gwinn had no idea who we were, but as he continued to fly over us, he began to see many others. He estimated that there were four groups scattered over a seventy-five mile area. The first group he believed consisted of about thirty; a second group about six miles away consisting of another forty; a third group about two miles from the second with perhaps as many as seventy-five; and a fourth group close by the third that consisted of about thirty-five. Gwinn's radio announcement was the first unwitting report of the USS *Indianapolis* disaster that later proved to be a key piece of information in solving the puzzle of the *Indy*'s second non-arrival report received at the naval operations base on the island of Leyte. 3.

As he continued to circle us, Gwinn once again returned to the antenna problem, solving it by reeling in the wire and affixing a rubber hose to it. He then sent a second message that read: SEND RESCUE SHIP 11-54 N 133-47 E 150 SURVIVORS IN LIFEBOAT AND JACKETS. 4. His urgent plea for help set into motion a rescue effort led by Lieutenant Adrian Marks who piloted a PBY-5A Catalina used for hunting subs and rescuing downed pilots. Marks later reached us at 3:20 P.M. He circled over a large area, dropping numerous kinds of provisions. Seeing this, I realized that there must be other survivors than just McKissick and myself, although we could not see them. Marks later indicated that as he circled over the men at about twenty-five to thirty feet, he could look into the emerald sea and detect hundreds of sharks swimming about. In fact, it was reported that just before Lt. Gwinn had arrived, an estimated thirty sharks had attacked approximately sixty boys clinging to a floater net, devouring them in a feeding frenzy within the span of about fifteen minutes. 5.

Open Sea Landing

The rescue attempt of Lt. Adrian Marks and his crew aboard the PBY was a tremendous act of heroism. The waves and wind were so fierce that afternoon that such an attempt was borderline suicidal. Yet in God's providence, Marks and his men saw the floating corpses and what appeared to be human remains. They saw men who were alive but in great peril—some even being attacked by sharks. I believe God compelled them to abandon their natural instinct for self-preservation to do His bidding by bravely landing that large craft in the open sea to bring us to safety. Historian Doug Stanton described what happened:

> "Speed was clearly of the essence. Marks skipped the usual communication protocol, sending an uncoded message back to Peleliu: BETWEEN 100 AND 200 SURVIVORS AT POSITION REPORTED X NEED ALL SURVIVAL EQUIPMENT AVAILABLE WHILE DAYLIGHT HOLDS X SURVIVORS MANY WITHOUT RAFTS.
>
> In the same message, Marks announced a bold decision: WILL ATTEMPT OPEN SEA LANDING. He had

never tried to land in the open sea before; all previous attempts by members of his squadron had ended in disaster. In fact, his squadron was now under standing orders that prohibited making them.

A few minutes later, he yelled into his crew's headsets, checking to make sure they agreed with his decision to attempt a landing. They gave him the thumbs-up. The team was going in. He cut the throttle, dramatically lifting the nose of the lumbering Catalina and setting her down in a power stall. Hitting the top of one wave, the *Playmate 2* was knocked back skyward fifteen feet. Then it came down even harder. At any moment, the plane could blow apart. On the third huge blow she settled down like a hen over an egg, her seams and rivets popping and seawater streaming in. Marks' crew shoved cotton and pencils into the holes in the metal skin of the plane. The radio compartment, located midplane, was taking on water, and the radioman began bailing immediately, starting a pace that would keep all the crew busy at a rate of ten to twelve buckets an hour. The propellers were still spinning, and it was essential that they didn't dig into the sea, or they would flip the plane.

Marks' copilot, ensign Irving Lefkovitz, moved to the side hatch and began preparing for rescue. Marks himself had no idea where to steer the plane; the whole craft pitched up and down as if on a carnival ride surrounded by rising and falling walls of water . . . The race was on to collect as many of the survivors as possible before total darkness consumed them all." 6.

I remember by the time I reached the raft that Lt. Gwinn had dropped for us, McKissick was gone. He had forsaken it and was already swimming toward the PBY that had landed several hundred yards from us. Although I could not see the plane, I could hear it. When I reached the deserted raft, it was upside-down. I immediately tried to turn it over and examine it to see if it had any drinking water on it. Finding nothing, I discovered an even greater setback. Due to a large hole, the raft could not be inflated. Then I understood why McKissick had abandoned it. In my frustration, I nearly stayed too long trying to make the raft usable.

By now McKissick was out of sight, headed for the rescue plane. I was sure that he would tell them that there was a Marine out there with him. As I quickly paddled my way in the direction of the sound of the engines, I began to realize that the plane was not stationary. It was slowly navigating its way through the valleys between the swells. I later learned that Marks was carefully trying to avoid contacting the massive walls of water with his wings while at the same time making his way toward possible survivors. Marks later described his dangerous maneuverings to the survivors:

"When we landed we realized that we couldn't rescue

everyone. We would have to make heartbreaking decisions. We would have to pick and choose among the survivors. From the air, we noticed that most of them were clustered into groups of ten or more men, clinging together. But, outside these groups, were many isolated swimmers, floating in their life jackets. Most of them were seemingly alive, but some were obviously already dead, including those whom we had seen being molested by sharks.

I decided that the men in groups stood the best chance of survival. They could look after one another, could splash and scare away the sharks, and could lend one another moral support and encouragement. But the single swimmers had no one else to turn to, and without the support of comrades, were the most likely to succumb to the despair of the night. Of course, I had no idea that you had been in the water for four and a half days! I therefore decided that we would concentrate on picking up the single swimmers, and the groups would have to wait for other rescue." 7.

Had I not been previously separated from my group, there is a strong possibility that I would not have been rescued that afternoon and would have had to wait until the next day when more help arrived. Such a prospect causes me to once again be awed by the unseen hand of divine providence that summoned me away from the group so I could later be among the first rescued. I'm sure I would not have survived the night. Lt. Marks described the horrific pathos of the rescue process indicating that men would wave and cheer as they saw him slowly taxi towards them. The crew would then enthusiastically wave back in recognition, and then deliberately pass them by to pick up the lone stragglers. Marks later lamented, "It was simply incomprehensible. They shouted and shook their fists and wept tears of black despair. And although they knew that they had been seen, the airplane never returned, and they were left to shiver through yet a fifth night until near morning when the *Doyle*'s boat finally found them." 8.

Eventually I saw the plane. With inexpressible joy I watched it come closer and closer. I had been spotted. I can still see the big wings of that PBY towering over me and hear the deafening sound of the massive engines turning the propellers. Before I knew it, someone pitched me a life ring on a rope. As I grabbed hold of the ring, I frantically tried to release my jacket but without success. I was too weak to free myself, especially given the force of being in tow by the plane. It felt as though they were going to pull me in half as they reeled me toward the plane while it was still moving. I was finally able to break the strings that tied my jacket together and slip it off. Once they pulled me up close to the plane, someone grabbed me and literally heaved me onto the plane. Unable to stand, the crewmen lifted me and carried me inside the plane. Being too weak to sit erect, they stacked me like a sack of feed up against the wall next to other wet and shivering survivors. It was obvious that we were all in the same condition. Covered with a filthy, greasy coat of oil, we all huddled together in a state that I can only describe as being somewhere between life and death. Warmed only by the body heat of unknown comrades, we were now united together by the inseparable bonds of combat survival.

I was happy to be alive, but too close to death to really appreciate what had just happened. I wasn't sure if I was dreaming, or if it was real. Hardly any talking was going on. Our tongues were swollen from dehydration and our bodies were fatigued beyond description. As God would have it, I looked across from me, and to my astonishment, the first person I recognized was my buddy Spooner. I saw his blond hair covered with oil and two protruding eyes that looked like massive sores of crimson red. Naturally, he could hardly see anything much less recognize me. One of the crewmen had given him a can of green beans and he was using his hands to feel for some kind of sharp object on the deck of the aircraft that he could use to open his precious container. I watched him for a few seconds, and suddenly he located a stud on the floor and began hacking away at it with the can, trying to knock a hole in it. Eventually he was successful and turned it up and began to drink the bean juice. I then said to him, "Hey Marine. How about sharing some of that with me?" At first he "politely" told me to leave him alone. But when I told him who I was, he lunged at me with a frenzied determination to share his prize.

As we embraced in that joyful reunion, I thanked God for

bringing to fulfillment my words to Spooner when earlier I had said, "Spooner, listen to me. There are only two Marines left in this group and when everyone else is gone, I'm still going to be here and you're going to be with me. I know in my heart that God is going to deliver us and we are going to survive this together."

Given my condition, combined with my limited ability to even see what was going on aboard the plane, I can only relate a very limited perspective of what actually happened over the next few hours. However, Lt. Marks painted a beautiful and comprehensive picture on the canvas of this divine recovery. His remarks have been inspirational to all of us who survived. He described the rescue operation as follows:

"I have known greatness in my time. When I landed my airplane, you had been swimming for eighty-seven hours. Our airplane carried four water breakers containing four and one-half gallons of fresh water each. Before the day ended, we were to take aboard so many men that this supply would figure only a little more than a quart each. As each exhausted survivor was hauled aboard, he was given half a cup of water. Then in three or four minutes, when his stomach had settled, he received half a cup more. Doubtless the first men rescued received a somewhat larger share of our supply than those rescued later, but after the first two drinks, they usually collapsed into a deep sleep, from which they only fitfully awakened to cry of thirst.

As the afternoon wore on, the hull of the old PBY was filled to capacity. There were two men in each bunk. We tried to sit them on the floor but they collapsed to lay two and three deep in every compartment of the airplane. It became absolutely impossible to walk through the airplane, and still each few minutes another desperately exhausted and ill survivor was being brought aboard.

Finally I shut off the engines and we started hauling men out on the wing. They were too exhausted to help themselves, and trying to balance ourselves on the bobbing airplane and pass these badly burned and helpless men up to the wing was a difficult, and sometimes dreadfully painful maneuver; but there wasn't any place else to put them. The wing, while broad enough had a decided slant toward the stern, so that it was necessary that each man be secured with a piece of parachute shroud line to prevent him from sliding off.

Darkness comes quickly in the tropics; and with the night we streamed a sea anchor from the bow and drifted. I had hoped to use our landing lights and an aldis lamp as a searchlight to continue our search for survivors, but we quickly found that plan to be impractical. An inventory disclosed that there was still some water left in one of the water breakers in the radio compartment. This water was passed up in a kettle, and someone groped his way through the darkness down the wings, giving each man half a cup. There never was very much water in the kettle because it trickled slowly from the spigot, and we didn't want to risk spilling a drop as we crawled along the wing of the pitching airplane. So, after four or five men had received their water ration, we crawled back to return the empty kettle and receive another with a few cups of water sloshing around in the bottom. Then we crawled back out (on) the wing and tried to determine where we had left off. And, as we passed these exhausted and dehydrated survivors, voice after voice in the darkness would say, "I've had mine," and that way we would find where we had left off, and go on down the wing with our ration of water. Fortunately the water lasted until we had delivered two rations down each wing, and although the men were still burning of thirst, no one ever took or asked (for) an extra ration." 9.

In total, Adrian Marks picked up fifty-six survivors that afternoon. As I lay there in that wet and slimy pile of quivering humanity, the comfort of a promise kept brought solace to my soul like a warm fire on a winter night. I knew that as surely as I was alive, God had been faithful to that which He had assured me when I first stepped into the black waters that first night. By the mercies of God, the darkness of that fourth night was vastly different from the three before. This night brought with it hope, not despair. Although my mind drifted in and out of a state of awareness, I do remember an overwhelming sense of worship and praise that flowed from the depths of my soul. My heart echoed the psalmist's words in Psalm 59:16 (KJV): "I will sing of thy power; yea, I will sing aloud of thy mercy in the morning: for thou hast been my defense and refuge in the day of my trouble." And had I been able to sing on that joyous night of rescue, my voice would have sounded forth the lyrics derived from that very text found in the great hymn, "I Sing the Mighty Power of God" written by Isaac Watts (1674-1748):

"I sing the mighty pow'r of God that made the mountains
    rise,
That spread the flowing seas abroad, and built the lofty
    skies.
I sing the wisdom that ordained the sun to rule the day;
The moon shines full at His command and all the stars obey.

I sing the goodness of the Lord that filled the earth with
    food;
He formed the creatures with His word and then pronounced
    them good.
Lord, how Thy wonders are displayed where'er I turn my
    eye:
If I survey the ground I tread or gaze upon the sky!

There's not a plant or flow'r below but makes Thy glories
known;

And clouds arise and tempests blow by order from Thy
throne;

While all that borrows life from Thee is ever in Thy care,

And everywhere that man can be, Thou, God, art present
there."

A Beacon of Hope

While nestled among my wet and shivering shipmates, clinging
to life in the darkness, I remember seeing the dim glow of a light
outside the plane. At first I didn't give it much thought; too weary
to even care. But after a while, the light grew brighter. Then someone—probably one of the crewmen—announced that the light
coming through the doorway was emanating from the destroyer
USS *Doyle* that was slowly but surely coming to get us. Knowing
this, that glow took on a new dimension. Its rays beamed a light of
hope that pierced the cold darkness of death. Speaking to survivors
some years later, Lt. Marks poignantly described this fascinating
phenomenon that occurred over the four to five hours we quietly
waited as the *Doyle* made its way to us:

"In an operation where so many things went wrong,

where so many people didn't get the word, and where many of those who did get it failed to appreciate the situation, the perception of Lt. Cdr. W. Graham Claytor in command of the *Doyle* was a shining exception. As he steamed through the gathering dusk, still more than a hundred miles away, he intercepted the radio conversation between me and the Ventura search plane. He knew that there might be enemy submarines ahead, because I had warned him of them, and he didn't know what sort of situation he was heading into; but he had the perception to know that somewhere up ahead men were clinging to life with their last ounce of strength, and that with darkness came cold, loneliness and despair. It is in the hours of darkness that most men give up the fight, and he felt that if there was something that he could do to give these men hope, to let them know that help was on its way, maybe they would summon the courage and the strength to hang on a few more hours.

I will never forget how dark were the early hours of that night. There was no moon, and the starlight was obscured by clouds. And even though we were near the equator, the wind whipped up and it was cold. We had long since dispensed the last drop of water, and scores of badly injured men, stacked three deep in the fuselage and ranged far out on both wings, were softly crying with thirst and with pain. And then, far out on the horizon, there was a light!

No matter the warning of submarines. No matter the unknown dangers of the night, the USS *Doyle* turned on her big twenty-four inch searchlight and pointed it straight up to reflect off the bottom of the clouds two thousand feet up in the sky. And it stayed on! For hour after hour it shone as a beacon of hope in the sky. The results on our own plane were electrifying. To the men who cried for water we would say, "Look! See that light! It's a destroyer on its way. There's water and doctors and rescue coming soon!" And men would settle back in hope to gaze upon that lovely light. And out around us, where men were struggling to survive their fifth night in the water, there were scores of you who saw the light and summoned up that one last ounce of strength to last till rescue came." 10.

Indeed, that light was a profound encouragement to us all. Certainly for me, and I'm sure many others, it was just one more reminder of the goodness of God. What a marvelous illustration of the Holy Spirit's words through the apostle James who reminds us that "Every good gift and every perfect gift is from above, and cometh down from the Father of lights, with whom is no variableness, neither shadow of turning" (James 1:17, KJV).

Words cannot describe those final hours of deliverance from out of the depths of the vast Pacific. I suppose the most profound realities of life are best described with complete silence. In fact, it took me over five years before I would even talk about the ordeal. It was simply too painful, yet also too sacred to mention. Even to this day, I can only bring myself to tell the story as a testimony to the glory and goodness of God. Having said that, perhaps the best depiction I have heard describing this supernatural scenario was the heart-rending summary given by Lt. Adrian Marks. Here's what he had to say many years later at one of the survivor reunions:

"I met you forty years ago. I met you on a sparkling, sun swept afternoon of horror. I have known you through a balmy tropic night of fear. I will never forget you. I suppose that through the years which have so swiftly run, at least ten thousand times I have recalled some portion of the day when our fates were crossed. But the memories which surface in my retrospection are not of horror, not of blackness, not of fear. I think of little things. Of things as small as honor, courage and as simple honesty. Things so small—and yet so great—that they form the cornerstone of our society. And when I think about these little things, I am humbled by the thought that I have seen true greatness in my time.

Some of my reflections have been so astonishing as to make me think of miracles. Sometimes we say that we are living in a world of miracles. Things beyond the wildest imagination of our forefathers are now every day experiences. We sit in our living rooms and watch events occurring half a world away. We bounce our messages off artificial moons which hang stationary in the sky. The computer which sits alongside my desk is a never ending source of astounding revelations to me. These miracles I have learned to accept, and even to understand. But there is a miracle which is beyond all of my powers of understanding. It is the miracle that you are here today, and not with your shipmates at the bottom of the Pacific Ocean.

What were the chances that you would be found? They were so minute as to be unbelievable. I flew many air sea rescue missions and I flew training missions where I searched for men who were deliberately placed out in the water to test various survival techniques. It was axiomatic that you could never find a lone man floating in the ocean. He could only be seen if he had some sort of survival aid. The best aid was a mirror. A mirror, catching the sun and flashing in the pilot's eye, was like the flash of a diamond. A package of dye marker made a great colorful glob on the surface of the water, which often could be found. The yellow color of a life raft was distinctive, and many times I went diving down in pursuit of a big yellow object, only to find that it was a cardboard box which had come unglued and was floating, spread out flat, upon the ocean. But you had none of these aids. You were simply out there, unknown and unmissed, floating in a dull gray life jacket which blended into the color of the water.

A man's head is about six inches wide and nine inches tall. If a pilot is flying a search mission, such as Wilbur Gwinn was flying at ten thousand feet, looking down at an angle of thirty degrees, what will he see? He will be looking down (at) an angle at the water about four miles ahead. The span of his vision will be about five miles. He will see twenty square miles at a glance.

How apparent will be the head of this man floating in the water? It will be about the diameter of the cross section of a human hair seen endwise across the room. It will be lost among the countless waves and whitecaps of the ocean. He simply won't be seen. And even if the pilot knew that somewhere out there a man was swimming, how could he search?

I turn to my computer. There are 6,080 feet in a nautical mile. There are 36,966,400 square feet in one square mile, three quarters of a billion square feet in one twenty square mile glance. And a floating man will occupy less than one square foot of that space. A search mission went out 600 miles. The air crew was supposed to make a visual search of ten miles on each side of this track. A radar search, such as Wilbur Gwinn was making, would be much wider.

I type these figures into my computer. 600 miles by twenty miles, 12,000 square miles on each pass. And it would take five passes to visually search a 100-mile wide strip. Multiply these figures, the computer overloads and goes into scientific notation. It can only write the figures in terms of exponents, and the very first exponent goes to the 12th power. Even the national debt starts to look small.

A pilot and his air crew normally look out at an angle at the water. They search the water for ships and the sky for aircraft. And the pilot won't see a man swimming in the water unless he happens to look right straight down on him. The only way you could be seen was for someone to look straight down on you. The only way a pilot can look straight down is to make a very steep banked turn, or to execute a dive bombing maneuver. And what pilot would do a silly thing like that in the forlorn and empty stretch of ocean where you were swimming?

What were the chances of that? What were the chances that Wilbur Gwinn would fly a course which would take him directly over you? What were the chances that his radio antenna would break while he was out on this mission? What were the chances that he would open his bomb bay doors and look straight down momentarily? And what were the chances that he would look straight down on one of you? You didn't have a chance in a million.

I know that most of you prayed a lot; and I know that some of you feel that it made a difference. Wilbur Gwinn is a wonderful man and a fine pilot. He never said that he heard a voice speak to him; but was there an unseen hand upon his shoulder? Did he find you by pure chance? The odds against it are one in a million—nay, one in a billion. But somehow he was chosen as the instrument to overcome these impossible, astronomical odds. Wilbur Gwinn looked down at the split second that would become one of the great moments of history. I, as well as you, am proud to know him as a friend.

Any sensible person knows that no one can swim for four and a half days; and yet you did. For forty years I have reflected upon the blind courage and the unbelievable greatness of spirit that I saw when each survivor was brought aboard my airplane, and I have been compelled by the evidence of my own eyes to believe in miracles." 11.

I agree. Our rescue was a marvel. But I would also hasten to add that my survival, along with that of my comrades, was not the ultimate purpose in such a supernatural event. No, whenever God performs any feat that arouses the awe and wonder of His creation, He does so primarily to bear witness to His own glory. And it is to that end I remain committed, for indeed, such a story has no human explanation. Only a sovereign, omnipotent God could have orchestrated such a scenario, for our good and His glory.

Chapter Seven

Tragedy and Triumph— the Fifth Day

⚓

Why are the nations in an uproar, and the peoples
devising a vain thing?
The kings of the earth take their stand, and the rulers
take counsel together against the LORD
and against His Anointed:
"Let us tear their fetters apart, and cast away
their cords from us!"
He who sits in the heavens laughs, The Lord scoffs at them.
Then He will speak to them in His anger and terrify
them in His fury:
"But as for Me, I have installed My King upon Zion,
My holy mountain."

. . . Now therefore, O kings, show discernment;

Take warning, O judges of the earth. Worship the

LORD with reverence,

And rejoice with trembling.

Do homage to the Son, lest He become angry,

and you perish in the way, for His wrath may soon be kindled.

How blessed are all who take refuge in Him!

Psalm 2:1-6, 10-12

In the late morning hours of the fifth night, we were finally rescued by the USS Bassett. *We will never forget the compassionate way the* Bassett *crew treated us. They placed each of the survivors on stretchers on the deck. They fed us warm liquids slowly to adjust our stomachs after having had nothing to eat or drink in four days and five nights. They washed us down with kerosene oil to remove the black crude oil that was on our bodies from head to toe. They even gave up their own clean, comfortable beds that we might get some much needed sleep for our weary bodies. They were true Samaritans to us. "Thanks,* Bassett *crew! We will never forget your kindness!"*

Survivor Concepcion P. Bernacil

I was in a group of 200-250 the first day. When we were picked up by Lt. Adrian Marks' PBY a few days later, there were only fifty-six men left in our group. The other shipmates were lost at sea. Later, we were transferred to the USS Doyle. *I would pray every day and every night for help that we would all make it home safely. I also prayed for the ones that we lost at sea. May God bless them and their families.*

Survivor Louis H. Erwin

One of my raftmates was preparing to amputate my lower leg to prevent gangrene, but we were rescued before any impromptu surgery had to be performed. My group was a handful of sailors picked up by the USS Register. *My leg was saved.*

Survivor Albert Ferguson

Only twelve survived in our group. There were sixteen of us when they dropped the life rafts, but four died before they picked us up. By that time, I was nothing but pus. My skin had blistered. I had gone from 130 lbs. to 80 lbs.

Survivor Verlin L. Fortin

The first ship wanted to give us encouragement, so it turned on its searchlights . . . one to the sky and one to the water. It was like an invitation to the Japanese. But you talk about a thrill seeing that! I am convinced that action saved some lives, because we then knew help was coming.

Survivor Earl W. Riggins

IT WAS NOW AROUND MIDNIGHT, Friday, August 3; four and one-half days after our ship had been sunk. The seas continued to churn while fifty-six survivors hung on for life aboard the disabled PBY. I had no idea how many other men were scattered for miles all around us, still clinging to life. With a mesmerizing rhythm, the billows swayed us back and forth under the clouds still glowing by the illumination of the approaching *Doyle*. There was great comfort in knowing the massive destroyer was steadily forging ahead to our rescue. It finally arrived on the scene at 11:45 P.M. some five hours after we were initially picked up. Over the next several hours we were transferred to the *Doyle* from the damaged PBY, nicknamed *Playmate 2*. At 12:30 A.M., the *Doyle* radioed the commander of the Western Carolines: HAVE ARRIVED AREA X AM PICKING UP SURVIVORS FROM THE USS INDIANAPOLIS (CA 35), TORPEODOED [*sic*] AND SUNK LAST SUNDAY NIGHT. 1.

I don't remember much about the transfer. I do, however, recall a net of some fashion being rolled over the side for us to climb up, but most were unable to do so. I vaguely remember being placed into a motor whaleboat that took a group of us to the ship. They fastened me into a wire basket of some sort and hoisted me aboard ship. After transferring our group of fifty-six aboard, the *Doyle* picked up another thirty-seven survivors that night for a total of ninety-three. By early dawn, their portion of the rescue was complete. Other ships gradually came, finding more sailors strewn over many miles. The following is a list of all the rescue ships that came to the scene on Friday, August 3. 2.

Ship Name	Arrival Time	Rescued
USS *Doyle* DE 368	0015	93
USS *Bassett* APD 73	0052	152
USS *Register* APD 92	0200	12
USS *Dufilho* DE 423	0300	1
USS *Madison* DD 425	0400	0
USS *Talbot* DE 390	0500	24
USS *Ringness* APD 100	1025	39

As the sun broke through the clouds that morning, the *Doyle* trained its guns on the crippled PBY and sent it to the bottom of the sea. It had been damaged severely in the landing, and was taking on a lot of water and leaking oil. By noon we were on our way to Peleliu, located 500 miles from the Philippines and about the same distance from New Guinea, an island that we had earlier taken from the Japanese. It was there that we lost over 10,000 marines and the Japanese lost an entire garrison of over 10,500 soldiers.

As we were being rescued, the B-29 crew of the *Enola Gay* was anxiously waiting for the skies to clear over their B-29 Base on Tinian so they could accomplish their mission. Their predetermined target was Hiroshima. I later learned that on the same day we were rescued, President Truman was returning to the United States from the Potsdam conference where he had met with Great Britain and Russia to strategize the final invasion plans to defeat Japan. While en route from London aboard the cruiser *Augusta*, he confidently informed reporters that America possessed a new weapon that could ultimately end the war. Obviously, the president was right. 3.

As I was taken aboard the *Doyle*, I recall two sailors wrapping my arms around their necks and literally dragging me to a compartment below deck. I remember my legs simply had no strength to hold me. Many of my shipmates were also in critical condition. Some had broken legs and arms, and many suffered excruciating pain from infected shark bites. They stretched me out on some kind of table, removed my clothes and began gently scrubbing the layers of oil off my skin with kerosene. Next they washed me with a salt-water soap, being extremely careful with those body areas that had rubbed together producing salt-water ulcers. All of my skin was basically decomposing and would peel off and bleed with the least bit of scrubbing. Later this proved to be a serious and miserable condition for all the survivors.

After I was cleaned up, my sympathetic attendants dressed me in a set of navy skivvies and placed me in one of the sailor's bunks. Another corpsman brought me some sugared water in a cup, but only allowed me to sip two or three tablespoons at a time.

After the *Doyle* dropped us off at Peleliu for about two days of medical attention, we were transferred aboard the hospital ship USS *Tranquility* on Monday morning, August 6. By about 1 P.M. we were on our way to the Naval Base Hospital 18 on Guam, arriving there on August 8. There they treated us for the painful salt-water ulcers along with other injuries. I vividly remember how they stretched out my arms and legs and cleaned off the infection—without any anesthetic. Not having any better treatment, they wrapped the ulcers in Vaseline gauze and strapped my limbs to the bed where I could not move. I was required to stay in this position for several days.

It was soon after arriving at the hospital in Guam that I had a visitor, one whom I had seen many times walking topside on the forward deck aboard the *Indianapolis*. It was Admiral Raymond Spruance. He had come to my bedside, pinned a Purple Heart on my pajamas top, thanked me for my service, wished me a good recovery, shook my hand and moved on to the next survivor. I was deeply moved by his sincerity and honored by his presence. Little did I know that that would be the extent of our recognition until the year 2001.

Shocking News

On August 6, while still in Peleliu, before our departure aboard the hospital ship *Tranquility,* a momentous event took place that would forever change the world; an event that remained a secret to all of the survivors for several days. While the providence of God was saving our lives, many other lives would be taken on that historic day. For it was on that day that the clouds over Tinian cleared and the *Enola Gay* finally departed with the *Indy*'s top-secret cargo secured in its bomb bay. Unknown to us, at 8:15 A.M., the first atomic bomb, nicknamed "Little Boy", was released over Hiroshima instantly killing more than 118,000 Japanese, and injuring another 140,000 who would ultimately die by the end of the year as a result of the explosion.

On Thursday, August 9, the second atomic bomb was dropped on Nagasaki. This one was nicknamed "Fat Man" and was responsible for killing 40,000 Japanese and seriously wounding another 60,000. The *Indianapolis* survivors knew nothing of what had happened. Nor did we know that on that same day, Admiral Chester Nimitz called from his headquarters just a few buildings from where we were recuperating for a court of inquiry to be opened concerning the sinking of the USS *Indianapolis.* In fact, even our loved ones did not know that we had been shipwrecked and rescued. The Navy was in full cover-up mode, a shocking story to be revealed in the next chapter.

The news of the detonation of the atomic bombs was finally revealed to us on August 10. It was then that we were able to put it all together. To our utter astonishment, we learned that the top-secret cargo we delivered to Tinian were the crucial components for the two bombs dropped at Hiroshima and Nagasaki. Obviously, the news media was buzzing around everywhere trying to get a special scoop on the story. I was interviewed by a reporter from the *Louisville Times.* I remember it well because I was still secured to my bunk, one of six Kentuckians that had survived. I still have the article, dated Aug. 15, 1945.

It was around this time that we learned that the Navy had waited two weeks after the sinking of the *Indianapolis* to make their first public announcement of the tragedy. Although we did not know it at the time, a cover-up was in the making and it took time to strategize a response that would stand up to both public and naval scrutiny in the days to come. This would ultimately be proven some fifty years later.

After about two weeks in the hospital, all the survivors were taken to a submarine camp to further convalesce. This was our first opportunity to get together since the rescue. For several days we all discussed the horrors we had experienced and mourned the loss of our shipmates who were not so fortunate. I was shocked when I discovered that only nine of my thirty-nine Marine companions aboard ship had survived. One of my most cherished possessions is a picture of all my fellow Marines under the massive barrels of number one turret with their signatures on the back of the picture.

It was a bittersweet reunion when I met with the other eight Marine survivors. I had seen some of them earlier while recuperating in sick bay, but now we were all together and able to discuss what had happened. In disbelief and with great sympathy, we talked about the thirty that perished and tried to determine if anyone was in their group at sea. Each of us had special buddies that we inquired about. We learned that our Captain Parke was so involved in swimming around his group—trying to keep them all together and defending them from the sharks—that he literally died of exhaustion. They said that his head finally collapsed into the water, never to rise again.

Our first sergeant, Jacob Greenwald, was not a swimmer, but said he got a lot of help, even a spare life jacket thanks to the help of another Marine survivor, Private Earl Riggins. He indicated that Earl had tied him to the center of the floater net to keep him safe. Everyone had stories that were unique to his group, both in how they survived the ordeal, and the vivid details of those who didn't.

We later learned of the gruesome recovery effort conducted on August 4 through 9 by four reconnaissance ships: the destroyers *Helm* (DD 388) and *Aylwin* (DD 355), and the destroyer escorts *French* (DE 367) and *Alvin C. Cockrell* (DE 366). After searching for hundreds of miles, the recovery effort was able to retrieve a total of ninety-one bodies for identification and burial. The tragedy and insanity of war is well illustrated in the report that was drafted by the *Helm*:

"All bodies were in extremely bad condition and had been dead for an estimated four or five days. Some had life jackets and life belts; most had nothing. Most of the bodies were completely naked, and the others had just shirts on. Bodies were horribly bloated and decomposed—recognition of faces would have been impossible. About half of the bodies were shark-bitten, some to such a degree that they more nearly resembled skeletons. From one to four sharks were attacking a body not more than fifty yards from the ship, and continued to do so until driven off by rifle fire.

For the most part it was impossible to get fingerprints from the bodies as the skin had come off the hands, or the hands were lacerated by sharks. Skin was removed from the hands of bodies containing no identification, when possible, and the Medical Officer will dehydrate the skin and attempt to make legible prints.

All personal effects [were] removed from the bodies for purposes of identification. After examination, all bodies were sunk, using two-inch line and a weight of three 5"/38 cal. projectiles. There were still more bodies in the area when darkness brought a close to the gruesome operations for the day. In all, twenty-eight bodies were examined and sunk." 4.

An acquaintance of mine, Dr. John Neumann, who was a member of the USS *Helm*, had charge of a burial detail of the men of the USS *Indianapolis*. Ironically, Neumann's most frightening experience with war and death occurred after the war had officially ended. He was among the Navy physicians called to recover the survivors and the floating dead after the sinking. He had this to say:

"I thought I had seen the worst, but it wasn't anything like recovering the bodies from the *Indianapolis*. As we prepared the dead for burial at sea, I saw so many dead sailors and Marines gutted apart. It was obvious that a shark had ripped off an arm or leg. The stench and the condition of the survivors as well as the dead, was very dreadful. Some of our (medical) team just couldn't take it and had to be replaced." 5.

The process of mourning was difficult for each of us. On the one hand, our hearts were filled with joy because we had survived; on the other hand, we felt twinges of guilt because we had not met the same fate as our comrades. Competing emotions were only complicated by the difficulties of our own physical and psychological wounds—some far deeper than we could have imagined—wounds that would fester for the rest of our lives.

Catastrophic Reflections

Our minds also reflected upon the inconceivable catastrophe caused by the bombs we had delivered. While no one rejoiced in such a calamity, we understood then, as we do now, that the devastation produced by the atomic bombs was merciful in comparison to the ongoing fire bombings that continued to incinerate the Japanese on a daily basis. One account indicates that in one night, 325 bombers destroyed sixteen square miles of Tokyo, killing 100,000 men, women and children and injuring untold thousands more. 6.

Relating a conversation he had with his pilot, one B-29 navigator named Tom Banks described what he saw firsthand during the summer of 1945:

"Pilot to Navigator, over."

"How far are we from the Japanese coast?"

"About ninety nautical miles."

"Better recheck, Navigator. We must be closer than that. Come up front and look."

As I knelt between the pilot and the copilot the pilot described an arc with his finger from far to the left to far to his right. The earth was on fire. No one spoke, I finally managed to mumble, "We're still ninety miles away."

As we approached the Japanese mainland, we could see that hell had been made real on the face of the earth. The ground below and everything on it was consumed by fire.

At the moment I wasn't debating the radical change in policy of the 20th Air Force—from high altitude missions against strategic military and industrial targets to low level fire raids. The objective was now simple: burn everything— plants, businesses, housing and people. As I glanced out my window I was awed by the unimaginable magnitude of the fire storm raging below. Nothing was distinguishable but colossal flames and boiling smoke.

Our airplane was now being buffeted by boiling air rising from the intense heat of the flames. Our two pilots struggled to maintain the aircraft reasonably level as our bombardier sought to identify his assigned bombing area. Finally the bombardier said, "My aiming point is in the middle of a huge fire—it's already been hit."

"Bombardier," the pilot ordered, "Pick out a spot some-where and start a new fire. Let's get rid of these bombs!" 7.

The religious fanaticism of the Japanese predisposed them to willingly die for their emperor—an inevitable reality had the war continued. While the death tolls from the atomic bombs were indeed staggering, had they not been dropped, causing Japan to surrender, these numbers would be multiplied many times by the continuation of the fire bombings alone. But these horrendous bombings pale into insignificance compared to what the Allies were planning to do next. Their plans for a full scale military invasion of Japan would have cost far more lives than those lost at Hiroshima and Nagasaki combined.

Top-secret military plans labeled Operation Downfall were later declassified, revealing plans for two massive invasions of Japan. On October 29, 1945, the 40th infantry division and the 158th Regimental Combat Team would invade and occupy a small island twenty-eight miles south of Kyushu where they would establish seaplane bases and a refuge for American carrier-based aircraft. This would precede an amphibious assault three days later on November 1, code named Operation Olympic. The British would land 1,500,000 combat troops, and the Americans would land 3,000,000 more. A second invasion, Operation Coronet, was scheduled to commence on March 1, 1946, delivering twenty-two combat divisions to destroy approximately 1,000,000 Japanese committed to defending the island of Honshu and the Tokyo Plain. General Willoughby, the chief of intelligence for General MacArthur, conservatively estimated American casualties to be around 1,000,000 by the fall of 1946. 8. One could only imagine the loss of life for the British and Japanese.

History records that President Truman had four alternatives for trying to end the war: 1) the use of the atomic bomb; 2) invasion of Japan (a two-phase operation.); 3) maintain blockades and continue conventional bombing; 4) negotiate a peaceful settlement. Obviously, President Truman chose the use of the atomic bomb because he was convinced that it would end the war quickly and save many hundreds of thousands of U.S. and British lives expected to be lost during the invasion. He also believed that the bomb would be a powerful deterrent that would help contain the expansionist agenda of the U.S.S.R. Although we can never know for certain, it would certainly appear that he was right on all accounts.

War is an amazing thing, an evil that defies description. Yet I am thankful that God has protected our great nation down through the years from murderous tyrants who have come against us. God has made it clear that "Whoever sheds man's blood, by man his blood shall be shed (Genesis 9:6), and "He who strikes a man so that he dies shall surely be put to death" (Exodus 21:12). Therefore, preemptive and retaliatory war is a necessary extension of capital punishment instituted by God to preserve innocent people from barbaric aggressors. God has established governments to serve and protect, "for it is a minister of God to you for good. But if you do what is evil, be afraid; for it does not bear the sword for nothing; for it is a minister of God, an avenger who brings wrath upon the one who practices evil" (Romans 13:4). The results of WWII give ample testimony to these truths.

Home at Last

The escort carrier *Hollandia* transported all of us from Guam back to San Diego. On September 26, over 300 survivors of the greatest naval catastrophe at sea arrived on the shores of the country they loved and served, only to be met with a paltry Salvation Army band. I cannot say that we knew what to expect, but we certainly thought there would be a more enthusiastic and official welcome. The rather large crowd on the pier had assembled to welcome home the crew of the *Hollandia* and knew nothing of the *Indianapolis* survivors. To my knowledge, none of our families or friends greeted us. Most did not even know our whereabouts. We remained on land as we were at sea—lost and neglected. We all had a mounting sense that we were somehow an embarrassment to the Navy, though at the time we did not understand why.

With no official welcome, we all came ashore and invisibly made our way through the crowd, somewhat envious of their jubilant and legitimate welcome for their loved ones. My eight Marine companions and I looked in vain for an official Marine reception that would at least transport us to the Marine Corp Base. Finally, we located an MP who helped us find a bus. I relate this story not to elicit sympathy, but only to underscore the realities that caused us all to become increasingly suspicious that something was wrong.

Someone has well said, "Truth and time walk hand in hand." Indeed, over the next few months we began to understand why we experienced such a mysterious cloud of concealment and disregard. The Navy was up to something. And the story of the *Indianapolis* had to stay out of the headlines until they had all their political ducks in a row.

Edgar Harrell, USMC
1945

Harrell family
Turkey Creek, Kentucky
(Ed, tallest boy in rear on left) 1940

Ed and Ola
Harrell
50th Wedding
Anniversary
1997

USS *Indianapolis* (CA-35), 1945
This is the last known photograph taken of the *Indianapolis*,
taken in Tinian Island harbor just after off-loading the world's
first operational atomic bombs.
Bureau of Ships Collection, U.S. National Archives

Charles Butler McVay III
Captain, USS *Indianapolis*
Edgar Harrell collection

USS *Indianapolis* (CA-35)
Edgar Harrell collection

USS *Indianapolis* under fire by Japanese shore batteries during the invasion of Saipan, June 1944.
U.S. Naval Historical Center

Invasion of Saipan, June 1944. Marine LVTs move toward the beach past bombarding cruisers on "D-Day", 15 June 1944. USS *Indianapolis* firing in the background.
U.S. Navy, National Archives

USS *Indianapolis* Marine Guard under number one turret. Ed directly under middle barrel, middle row. 1945
Edgar Harrell collection

Signatures on back of photo of Marine Guard
under number one turret. 1945
Edgar Harrell collection

USS *Indianapolis* antiaircraft guns firing at approaching kamikaze plane. 1945
Edgar Harrell collection

Japanese kaiten; the Japanese human torpedo.
Edgar Harrell collection

Japanese Lieutenant
Commander Mochitsura
Hashimoto at the periscope
of his submarine, the *I-58*.
Edgar Harrell collection

The Japanese submarine *I-58* that torpedoed and sank the
USS *Indianapolis*.
U.S. Marine Corps Photograph.

USS *Indianapolis*
survivors en route
to a hospital follow-
ing their rescue.
Ambulance in the
background is
marked "U.S.N.
Base Hospital No.
20", located on
Peleliu.
U.S. Navy Photograph,
National Archives.

USS *Tranquility*
(AH-14) arrives at
Guam, carrying
survivors of
USS *Indianapolis*,
8 August 1945.
U.S. Navy Photograph,
National Archives

USS *Indianapolis*
survivors brought
ashore from USS
Tranquility at Guam,
8 August 1945. They
are being placed in
ambulances for
immediate transfer to
local hospitals.
U.S. Navy Photograph,
National Archives.

Nine Marine survivors of the USS *Indianapolis*. Top row (left to right): Miles Spooner, Earl Riggins, Paul Uffelman, Giles McCoy, Melvin Jacob; Bottom row (left to right): Max Hughes, Raymond Rich, Jacob Greenwald, Edgar Harrell. 1945
Edgar Harrell collection

Five Marine survivors
(left to right):
Earl Riggins, Jacob
Greenwald, Melvin
Jacob, Edgar Harrell,
Giles McCoy. 2002
Edgar Harrell collection

Airport reception for first reunion. Captain McVay (white suit
and hat) shaking hands with Edgar Harrell (with Harrell's wife
Ola to his right).1960
Edgar Harrell collection

At the 45th survivor's reunion, Edgar Harrell (left) with his
shipmate, Charles McKissick, the last man alive in his group
before rescue.1990
Edgar Harrell collection

The USS *Indianapolis* (CA-35) Survivors Memorial
Organization designed, erected and financed the
USS *Indianapolis* (CA-35) National Memorial in honor
of the ship and her crew, dedicated on August 2, 1995.
Edgar Harrell collection

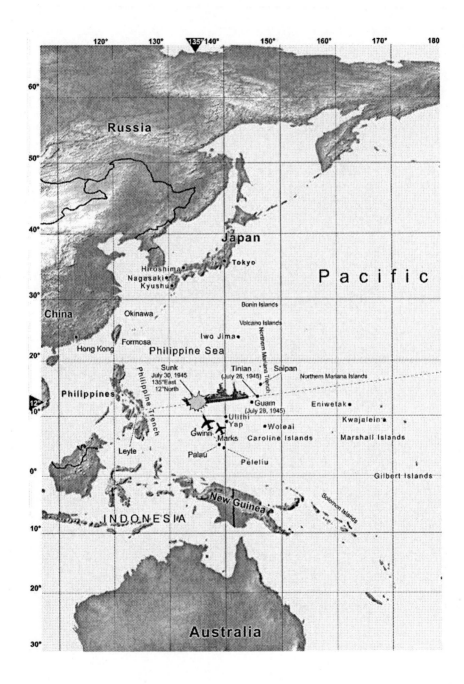

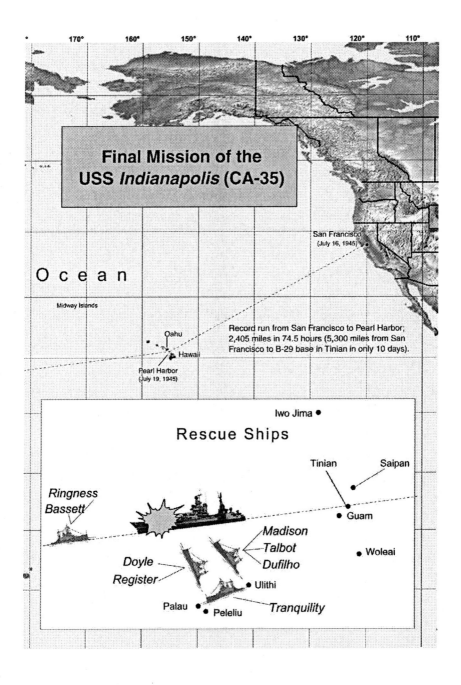

Final Mission of the USS *Indianapolis* (CA-35)

San Francisco (July 16, 1945)

Ocean

Midway Islands

Oahu

Record run from San Francisco to Pearl Harbor; 2,405 miles in 74.5 hours (5,300 miles from San Francisco to B-29 base in Tinian in only 10 days).

Hawaii

Pearl Harbor (July 19, 1945)

Iwo Jima

Rescue Ships

Tinian   Saipan

Ringness
Bassett

Guam

Madison
Talbot
Dufilho

Woleai

Doyle
Register

Ulithi

Palau
Peleliu

Tranquility

Chapter Eight

Journey for Justice

⚓

Open thy mouth, judge righteously,
and plead the cause of the poor and needy.
Proverbs 31:9, KJV

On the first day, our hopes were high about being rescued. Weren't we expected in Leyte? Weren't we to have a plane come out with a sleeve for gunnery practice? We thought it would not be long. Little did we know no one was looking for us. We just vanished. To this day, I can't believe than an admiral with a staff of a hundred men did not question where his flagship was when it did not arrive. Too much was ignored and forgotten. Why did so many men have to die?

Survivor Victor R. Buckett

To what do I attribute my survival? To me it wasn't luck. The God of my salvation was with me and delivered me. Not what I deserved, by any means, but the grace of God to be usable in his service. I've been trying to serve him by being a pastor and teaching for a long time . . . remembering how thankful I should be just to be alive and back home with my family.

Survivor Granville S. Crane Jr.

I always will have great respect for Captain McVay. I believe he was correct in his decision. If it were possible, I would serve under him again and be very happy to do so.

Survivor Claudus Evans

It is a shame that after working so long to clear our skipper's name and combat record it has taken a fourteen-year-old boy—God love him—to finally get the attention of the Congress and to have this joint resolution introduced. Now that we have this chance at last I urge you to pass Senate Joint Resolution 26 before all of us, the survivors, have died and joined our shipmates still at sea.

Survivor Giles G. McCoy 1.

I and several other men were in Washington to testify on behalf of our Captain. We knew that he was getting a real raw deal from the navy, but to our disbelief, he was unfairly court-martialed anyway. While waiting in the hallway outside the courtroom, we watched as marine guards escorted in a Japanese man. We were shocked to learn later that the Japanese man we had seen was Lt. Commander Hashimoto of the submarine that had sunk our ship. And unbelievably, the navy had had him brought there to testify against Captain McVay!

Survivor Kenley M. Lanter

Yes, I am mad they didn't pick us up. If you go on leave or liberty and you're ten minutes late, you are court-martialed. But here is a ship, a quarter of a mile long, weighing ten thousand tons, with twelve hundred people . . . the thing is missing for days, and nobody looks for it. Yes, I am still bitter about that. I feel sorry for the guys that died. I figured maybe the good Lord had his arm around me.

Survivor James F. Newhall

⚓

W HILE OTHER NAVAL VESSELS WERE ALSO SUNK as a result of combat during the war, only the *Indianapolis* met her fate while leaving the enemy that sunk her completely unscathed. Worse yet, it was estimated that only one-third of the casualties suffered were a result of the initial attack. The other two-thirds were victims of Navy incompetence—a series of debacles that placed us in harm's way unescorted, and ignored our SOS, forcing hundreds of men to fend for themselves in the open sea. A disaster now considered the greatest naval catastrophe at sea in the history of the U.S. Navy. Because of their radical commitment to avoid culpability, the Navy concealed many facts that would indict them. Instead, the blame was placed upon our skipper. As in most politics, spin and selective reasoning typically exonerate the guilty and indict the innocent. Such was the case with Captain McVay. Unfortunately, the truth would not be fully disclosed to the public for over fifty years when Navy documents were finally declassified and various individuals began to come together searching for truth and justice.

On Monday, August 13, 1945, the court of inquiry convened according to Admiral Nimitz's orders. Knowing that news of the sinking would eventually reach the public and desiring to know the facts, the Navy needed some answers and they needed them fast. At this point, they were still unclear about how we were sunk. The scuttlebutt even included the rumor that we hit a mine. With so many of the recuperating survivors scattered in Guam, Leyte, Peleliu, and Samar, it was virtually impossible to gather all the facts. Although the inquiry board conceded that they "were starting the proceedings without having available all the necessary data," that did not stop them from convening and asking many pertinent questions. They needed to know what caused the disaster, why the delay in rescue, who was at fault and were there any violations of military laws. Out of the fifteen officers and 301 enlisted men that survived, only the testimonies of Captain McVay, four other officers and fifteen enlisted men were heard. Historian Dan Kurzman described the fascinating account of the inquiry in his book, *Fatal Voyage*:

"The military witnesses were called to testify one by one, and the sphere of responsibility was tossed from one officer to the next as if it were a football loaded with dynamite. Officers of the Philippine Sea Frontier Command took the stand: Commodore Gillette, Captain Granum, Lieutenant Commander Sancho, and Lieutenant Gibson. CINCPAC was at fault, they charged, for although it issued an order not to report arrivals of combatant ships, it never mentioned what to do about nonarrivals—so it was "naturally" assumed that they shouldn't be reported either. Sancho, at the same time, pointed out that Gibson, his subordinate, had never told him that the *Indianapolis* was overdue.

Commodore Carter of CINCPAC answered the PSF witnesses: True, an order about nonarrivals had not been issued, but as a matter of common sense they should have been reported by Gibson's office as well as by Admiral McCormick's command. Admiral McCormick of Task Group 95.7 also lobbed the ball back to the PSF officers: Why didn't they keep track of the ship? He himself would have done so, but the cable informing him that the *Indianapolis* was to train under his command was incorrectly decoded by members of his staff and was never delivered to him. Not his fault, of course.

Officers of the Marianas Command, Captain Naquin and Lieutenant Waldron, claimed innocence, too, and were not pressed. Their commander, Admiral Murray, was, of course, one of the judges. Yes, Naquin agreed, he did have information about the four submarines on an offensive mission and the sinking of the *Underhill*, but he still thought that the threat was "negligible." Waldron also thought the threat was negligible—for Naquin never told him about those submarines or the sinking. No one ashore, it seemed, shared any responsibility for the tragedy." 2 .

The Need for a Scapegoat

As the proceedings dragged on, Captain McVay struggled with pessimism. His reputation was at stake, perhaps even his career. Although he had not yet been charged with any dereliction of duty, he knew the Navy would need a scapegoat. Naturally, he feared it would be him. However, as the inquiry drew to a close, McVay declined to make a closing argument. After all, to his surprise and relief, he had not been indicted in any way. In fact, by the end of the inquiry, his pessimism had changed to optimism as he believed that ultimately the Navy's much needed blame would fall where it rightfully should—squarely on the shoulders of those on shore. Unfortunately, however, that is not the way things turned out. Again, historian Dan Kurzman recounts the appalling conclusion to the inquiry:

"A court-martial seemed out of the question. America had lost over seven hundred ships in the war, and not one of their skippers had been court-martialed. The judges, no doubt, realized that if they were to single him out, it would be obvious that the Navy was looking for a scapegoat.

McVay thus dared to hope that the velvet-gloved treatment he had so far received at this hearing was a presage of lenience for him, and he was unshaken even when the judge advocate stated unequivocally: 'Any officer found negligent should be punished!'

But then, as he sat in the hearing room for the last time, he was shocked to learn that the velvet gloves had an abrasive lining. The judge advocate was piling "fact" upon "fact," building up to a set of "false" conclusions:

- Lieutenant Waldron had warned him of the submarine menace, and yet the captain did not zigzag on the fatal night.
- Visibility was good on that night, making it even more essential for him to zigzag.
- He delayed sending out an SOS message.

McVay sat quietly, listening in disbelief. 'The judge advocate was wrong on all three counts!' he cried to himself in bitter rage.

Despite his fury and dismay, McVay clung to a straw of optimism as the court began apportioning the blame. It recommended: That Lieutenant Gibson be sent a Letter of Admonition, a lesser censure than a reprimand, for failing to report the nonarrival of the *Indianapolis* in Leyte; and that

Admiral McCormick be ordered to discipline his staff for not decoding the cable that explained why the *Indianapolis* would be reporting to him.

Although McVay felt that Gibson and McCormick's men, whatever their own responsibility, were being made scapegoats for their gold-braided superiors, the judges, by recognizing that people ashore had made blunders, might conclude that the skipper wasn't responsible for the disaster. Still, this could be wishful thinking, he realized, and the court might well recommend that he, too, be given a letter of censure, demolishing his career, as he had long anticipated.

McVay's surge of optimism *was* wishful. The captain listened in shock as a judge rasped out the court's recommendation in his case: Not only should he receive a Letter of Reprimand, but he should be brought to trial by general court-martial for performing his duties inefficiently and endangering lives through his negligence." 3.

Helplessness and Disbelief

The die was now cast for our skipper's fate. As news about the inquiry trickled down to the survivors, we all felt his pain. There was a strange cloud of disbelief, even betrayal that hovered over us. Suddenly we all had become victims of a profound injustice. It was not just the captain being maligned, but because of our loyalty to him, we all felt attacked. How, after all we had been through, could they possibly come to such a conclusion? Over seven hundred ships had been sunk during the war and not one captain had been court-martialed. We were at a complete loss to understand their reasoning. The same helpless feelings of being adrift at sea began to grip our hearts again as we felt abandoned once more by the Navy and powerless to do anything about it.

As I recuperated in the Marine Corps Base Hospital in San Diego, I reflected upon the captain we all so deeply admired. I would often replay the scenes of that horrific night. And every time I relived those moments, hearing the screams, feeling the explosions, and stepping into the oil-laden water, I could never determine anything that would place blame upon the skipper. It simply made no sense to me, nor my shipmates. My frustration finally motivated me to write the captain. This is what I wrote:

December 9, 1945

Dear Captain McVay,

I've been reading about the court-martial they've been trying to pull in Washington, and I must say I think it very absurd. I've read the testimonies given by some of the crew members, and if I can offer any help, I would be more than glad to do so.

I know personally the word was passed orally to abandon ship. Also I believe that as many as nine hundred crewmen left the ship, and the remaining compliment were trapped below decks or killed instantly. Most of these were in sick-bay country and in the two compartments below.

I'm now at M.C.B. waiting discharge.

Respectfully yours,

Corp. Edgar Harrell

Captain McVay kindly responded to my offer in the following correspondence:

December 14, 1945

Corp. Edgar A. Harrell

Unit 3 Casual Platoon

R & R. Center, M.C.B.

San Diego, California

Dear Harrell:

Thank you very kindly for your letter of December the ninth, which reached me yesterday. I appreciate greatly your offer to testify that you personally heard the order to abandon ship, and should I feel it necessary to call you to Washington, after your offer, I will not hesitate in doing so. Since all the surviving officers and many of the men are now here, I believe that we have enough witnesses to place all the facts before the Court.

There are two of your Detachment here now, McCoy and Rich, but if I need your backing, I will ask them to order you on.

Again, many thanks for your offer.

Very sincerely yours,
Chas. B. McVay, 3rd
Captain, U.S. Navy

As bereaved family members of deceased sailors and Marines learned of the fatal sinking, they demanded answers. Human nature naturally looks for someone or something to blame when great tragedy strikes. Unfortunately, many families blamed the captain for their loss. At some level this was understandable, because they did not have the facts. The hate mail and death threats came pouring in—a most unfortunate burden for the captain to bear.

Trial by General Court-Martial

The trial began on December 3, 1945. The secretary of the Navy, James Forrestal, brought two charges against him. The first being, "negligence suffering a vessel of the Navy to be hazarded." Specifically stated: "In that Charles B. McVay, 3rd, captain, U.S. Navy, while so serving in command of the USS *Indianapolis*, making passage singly, without escort, from Guam, Marianas Islands, to Leyte, Philippine Islands, through an area in which enemy submarines might be encountered, did, during good visibility after moonrise on 29 July 1945, at or about 10:30 P.M., minus nine and one-half zone time, neglect and fail to exercise proper care and attention to the safety of said vessel in that he neglected and failed, then and thereafter, to cause a zigzag course to be steered, and he, the said McVay, through said negligence, did suffer the said USS *Indianapolis* to be hazarded, the United States then being in a state of war." 4.

The second charge against him was, "culpable inefficiency in the performance of duty." Specifically stated: "In that Charles B. McVay, 3rd, captain, U.S. Navy, while so serving in command of the USS *Indianapolis*, making passage from Guam, Marianas, to Leyte, Philippine Islands, having been informed at or about 12:10 A.M., minus nine and one-half zone time, on 30 July 1945, that said vessel was badly damaged and in sinking condition, did then and there fail to issue and see effected such timely orders as were necessary to cause said vessel to be abandoned, as it was his duty to do, by reason of which inefficiency many persons on board perished with the sinking of said vessel, the United States then being in a state of war." 5.

Not only were the charges brought against captain McVay contrived machinations of political blame-shifting, but the proceedings were also highly unusual, further betraying a hidden agenda. To everyone's astonishment, the Navy ordered Japanese submarine Commander Hashimoto, the man who sunk the *Indy*, to be called from Japan as a witness against the captain. This was unprecedented in the history of the Navy. It was an unconscionable aberration of justice for the United States to place an enemy in a position to accuse one of our own patriots. It is interesting to note, however, that Hashimoto's testimony actually worked in favor of the captain's defense in that he indicated that it would have made no difference whether the ship was zigzagging or not. Given all the conditions on that fateful night, his torpedoes would have hit the ship regardless.

Ultimately, the Navy found McVay guilty of the first charge, failure to zigzag, and not guilty of the second charge, failure to issue the order to abandon to ship. The court sentenced him to lose 100 numbers in both his temporary rank of captain and in his permanent rank of commander. Interestingly, his final fitness report record read: "This record contains only one unfavorable entry, a Letter of Reprimand concerning the loss of the USS *Indianapolis*, but otherwise this record of the accused deserves the rating of outstanding during his entire commissioned service." 6.

The Navy's blunders were now safely concealed in the archives, well hidden from the discerning eye of the public. They had sacrificed our skipper on the altar of Navy pride. Personal vengeance also seemed to fuel the injustice against the captain. Evidently, one very influential father, Thomas D'Arcy Brophy, was so grieved over the loss of his son Tom Brophy, that he set out on a personal crusade to seek revenge upon the man whom he believed was responsible for his son's death—Captain McVay. Testimonies later indicated that Brophy used his formidable political influence to pressure Secretary Forrestal, and even his friend President Truman, to do all they could to destroy McVay. 7.

No doubt they were confident that his innocence would never rise again from the grave to haunt them. While the verdict could have been worse, it was, nevertheless, the end of Captain McVay's noble career. In an effort that would now seem to be an attempt to alleviate a guilty conscience, his commendations and awards were also included into the record, namely: "twenty-six years and the Silver Star 'for conspicuous gallantry and intrepidity' in the Solomon Islands campaign, the Bronze Star with combat V for the Okinawa assault, the Purple Heart and the Asiatic-Pacific Campaign Medal with four bronze stars." 8.

Later, in 1946, Secretary Forrestal remitted Captain McVay's sentence and restored him to duty, largely due to the recommendation of Admiral Nimitz who had become Chief of Naval Operations. The good captain then served his remaining time in the

New Orleans Naval District where he retired in 1949 with the rank of Rear Admiral.

The Birth of the Survivor's Organization

During this time, the survivors' conviction of Captain McVay's innocence continued to fester like an unrelenting boil. Our desire to see him completely exonerated gradually took shape over the next several years. In 1958, an editor of the Associated Press and former wartime naval correspondent in the Pacific, Richard F. Newcomb, wrote the first book detailing the sinking, entitled, *Abandon Ship!* For all the survivors, Newcomb's accounting only added fuel to the fire of vindication as his research gave further clarity to the miscarriage of justice.

During this period, Marine survivor McCoy was also busy writing letters and making phone calls in an effort to contact survivors and organize a reunion as well as a strategy to help exonerate the captain. After a Herculean effort on his part, 220 of the 317 survivors were located and invited to our first reunion on July 30 and 31, 1960, held in Indianapolis, Indiana. Finally, after fifteen years, we were all reunited and organized to once again go into battle for Captain McVay.

In the initial stages of organization, I met with several survivors including McCoy and was asked to be program chairman for the first reunion. One of my responsibilities was to invite Captain McVay to come as our guest of honor and speak to us. With that in mind, I sent him the following letter:

November 28, 1959

Vice Admiral Charles B. McVay, III
1527 Fourth Street
New Orleans, Louisiana

Admiral McVay, please – Program Chairman Edgar Harrell writing.

A group of USS *Indianapolis* survivors met in Indianapolis, Indiana on October 3rd and 4th. The purpose was for working toward a complete organization of a reunion for all fellow survivors of our ship.

With the wonderful assistance of the many city officials of Indianapolis, our reunion is to be a reality. It will be held July 30th and 31st, 1960 in the city of Indianapolis, Indiana.

In brief the program consists of the normal procedures leading up to a banquet on Saturday evening. On Sunday a special war memorial service will be conducted at the Indianapolis war memorial building.

As program chairman, we would like to extend to you a

very special invitation to be guest speaker at our banquet. We realize this is in the distant future, but certainly would like your reply as soon as possible.

Should you desire more information regarding other activities or details, I would be more than glad to supply this information to you.

Very truly yours,

Edgar Harrell
Program Chairman

Captain McVay replied as follows:

8 December, 1959

Mr. Edgar Harrell
Pella Rolscreen Company
520 24th Street
Rock Island, Illinois

Dear Mr. Harrell:

Your letter of November 28th has been received. Please do

not reserve more than fifteen minutes for my talk. I feel certain that is sufficient time for anyone at such a function.

Please give me more information regarding other activities and send me details on the two-day reunion as they become available.

Very truly yours,
Chas. B. McVay, 3rd
Rear Admiral, U.S. Navy (Ret.)

When the long-anticipated day finally arrived, most of the 220 men and their wives gathered together at the airport to greet our dear captain. Approximately 500 people formed a line in his honor. In shock, he and his wife Louise exited the plane and tearfully made their way past the sailors and Marines who stood at full attention, saluting him with tears streaming down their cheeks. It was a grand and glorious sight. He later acknowledged that he was somewhat concerned about how he would be received, given the disgraceful reprimand at the general court-martial. Certainly, with the relentless barrage of hate mail he received from devastated families, he was predisposed to thinking the worst. But to his great joy, he was received with utmost respect and military dignity. After all, we knew he was innocent.

The joy and triumph of our reunion, however, were short-lived.

In 1961, his faithful wife Louise was diagnosed with cancer and died. A few years later, in 1965, his beloved grandson died. For reasons no one will ever know, Captain McVay became convinced that life was no longer worth living. Consequently, in November 1968, he walked out onto his front porch, put a revolver to his temple, and ended his life on earth.

The news of his death, though painful, only fanned the flames of our resolve to see him exonerated. Our dedicated chairman of the survivor's organization, Marine Giles McCoy, pressed harder and harder to correct the injustice. By then, several books on the sinking of the *Indianapolis* were in print, each one painting a dark cloud over the Navy and the way they had treated an excellent captain. Every five years the survivors would have another reunion. And every time we met, we continued in our commitment to push forward at all cost to see him cleared of all blame. We even refused a Navy Presidential Citation as a protest against his mistreatment.

Justice at Last

Finally, in the providence of God, we began to see a light at the end of this very long tunnel of injustice and political stonewalling. Hunter Scott, a sixth-grade elementary school student from Pensacola, Florida, had been inspired by the motion picture "Jaws" where an actor played the role of a USS *Indianapolis* survivor.

Although I have not personally seen the movie—I avoid anything that reminds me of the horrors we experienced—evidently the "survivor" vividly described our plight in the shark-infested waters. Intrigued with the story, the young boy wanted to learn more. After conferring with his father, he decided to research the story and enter his findings in a sixth grade history fair.

In his article, *Timeline to Justice*, Hunter Scott provides an excellent summary of the evidence that he discovered that was instrumental in exonerating Captain McVay. There he writes, "After two years of research and interviews with almost all remaining *Indianapolis* survivors, I have amassed what one naval historian has called 'the greatest collection of information on the USS *Indianapolis* in the world.' On 22 April 1998, accompanied by Congressman Joe Scarborough (R-FL), Congresswoman Julia Carson (D-IN), and 11 *Indianapolis* survivors, I personally dropped H.R. 3710 into the hopper on the floor of Congress. This bill will erase all mention of the court-martial and conviction from the record of Captain Charles B. McVay III and award a Presidential Unit Citation to the USS *Indianapolis* and her crew." 9.

The following timeline summary, compiled by Hunter Scott, exposes the Navy cover-up with startling clarity.

"Based on my research, the following timeline tells the story of the final days of the *Indianapolis*.

- 16 July 1945—Robert Oppenheimer and General Leslie Groves choose to load components for the first atomic bomb on board the *Indianapolis*. Captain McVay receives orders to proceed 'with all possible haste' to Tinian.

- 21 July—The USS *Underhill* (DD-682) is sunk by a Japanese submarine in the same area where the *Indianapolis* will go down. Captain McVay never is given this information nor any notification that the Japanese submarines *I-58* and *I-367* are operating in the area. A directive from the Chief of Naval Operations, Fleet Admiral Ernest J. King, prevents Captain McVay from receiving this intelligence.

- 26 July—The *Indianapolis* arrives in Tinian; atomic bomb components are unloaded. Captain McVay receives orders to proceed to Guam, then to Leyte for gunnery practice with the USS *Idaho* (BB-42) on 2 August. The *Idaho* receives a garbled message about the arrival of the *Indianapolis*. No request is made for retransmission. The *Idaho* is unaware that the *Indianapolis* is en route. (This is the first in a series of blunders that led the *Indianapolis* to cruise into a bureaucratic void.)

- 28 July—In Guam, Captain McVay is denied requests for an escort. His orders give him discretion concerning whether or not to zigzag while under way. The *Indianapolis* makes the trip from Guam to Leyte unescorted—the first heavy warship to do so during the war—without capabilities to detect enemy submarines.

- 31 July—At sunset, Captain McVay comes on the bridge to discuss weather conditions. The night is overcast and cloudy. He believes he is cruising in waters free of enemy submarines, because of intelligence given to him prior to his departure from Guam. The *Indianapolis* is doing seventeen knots, and Captain McVay gives orders to cease zigzagging because of poor visibility. He gives orders to be awakened if weather changes occur.

- 1 August—At 0004, the ship is struck by two of six torpedoes fired by the *I-58*. The first torpedo takes off sixty feet of her bow, and the second hits amidships, igniting the powder magazine and shutting off most electrical power. Chief Radio Electrician L. T. Woods, observed by Radio Technician 2nd Class Herbert J. Minor, sends SOS and position of the *Indianapolis* on 500 kilocycles from Radio Room II, which maintains power. According to Minor, at least three signals are transmitted. Former Yeoman 2nd Class Clair B. Young stated in a letter received by Commander T. E. Quillman, Jr., 'while stationed at U.S. Navy 3964 Naval Shore Facilities Tacloban, Philippine Islands, that he personally delivered the SOS message to Commodore Jacob H. Jacobson, U.S. Navy.'

Young awakens Commodore Jacobson and notices a strong odor of alcohol in the room. Commodore Jacobson reads the message, which identifies the ship, her location, and her condition. Mr. Young asks Commodore Jacobson: 'Do you have a reply, sir?' The answer comes: 'No reply at this time. If any further messages are received, notify me at once.' The SOS is received and ignored. Meanwhile, Commander Hashimoto of the *I-58* radios Japan and indicates that he has just sunk a battleship and gives the location. The message is decoded by the U.S. Navy. Still, no one checks on the whereabouts of the *Indianapolis*.

- 2 August—The *Indianapolis* is due to arrive in Leyte that morning. Upon non-arrival, the ship is taken off the plotting board, and no effort is made to determine where she is. Admiral King had standing orders that combatant ships' arrivals in port were not to be reported, which implied that non-arrivals also were not to be reported.

- 3 August—Lieutenant Wilbur Gwinn, flying a Ventura bomber, accidentally spots *Indianapolis* survivors and radios Palau for rescue operations to commence. Lieutenant Adrian Marks lands a PBY in heavy seas and picks up fifty-six survivors. Tom Brophy defies orders and tries to swim to the plane; he does not survive.

- 4 August—Rescue operations start in a fifty-mile radius.

- 6 August—First atomic bomb is dropped on Hiroshima.

- 15 August—Japan surrenders. Navy releases information about the sinking of the *Indianapolis*. The press begins to ask the Navy why the ship was never missed.

NOTE: The father of the aforementioned Tom Brophy goes to Washington after the war to arrange a meeting with Captain McVay. According to Mr. D. J. Blum, Brophy tries to call on Captain McVay the day he arrives in Washington and is told to arrange the meeting for the following week because of Captain McVay's prior commitments.

Brophy follows Captain McVay, who attends a party. Furious, Brophy meets with his friend, President Harry S. Truman, and convinces him to court-martial Captain McVay. President Truman pressures Admiral King to convene a court-martial. Admiral King himself appoints the members of the court, who know Admiral King wants Captain McVay found guilty and who also are depending upon Admiral King for promotions.

- 3 December—Court-martial begins. Captain McVay requests Lieutenant Commander Donald Van Koughnet, Chief Legal Officer of the U.S. Navy Military Government for the Marianas Islands, to represent him. Admiral King denies the request. The charges are 'failure to follow a zigzag course' and 'failure to sound an abandon ship.'

NOTE: Since 1991, several Navy documents have been declassified, showing that Captain McVay was not given intelligence that could have prevented this disaster (see 'ULTRA and the Sinking of the USS *Indianapolis*,' a paper given to the Eleventh Naval History Symposium, 1993). This same information—which could have been useful in Captain McVay's defense, showing that the 'super technical' charges were unfounded—was considered top-secret in 1945 and was not used in the court-martial. The question as to why the men of the *Indianapolis* spent five nights and four days in the water without anyone noticing that the ship was missing was not considered in the trial.

- 13 December—Admiral King brings in Hashimoto, commander of the *I-58* to testify against Captain McVay. Hashimoto states that zigzagging would have made no difference, that he would have sunk the *Indianapolis* anyway. The *I-58* had several kaitens on board, had the six-torpedo spread missed its target. The *Indianapolis* was doomed.

- 19 December—Captain McVay found guilty of failure to follow a zigzag course, therefore hazarding his ship. His sentence, loss of 100 promotion numbers, is later remitted. His conviction is not. The guilty verdict stands to this day. Out of more than 700 ships lost in World War II, the *Indianapolis* is the only one to have her captain court-martialed.

- 6 November 1968—Captain McVay commits suicide.

NOTE: In a 10 August 1990 letter to Senator Richard

Lugar (R-IN), Captain Russell E. Sullivan stated that he was on board the USS *General R. L. Howze* (AP-134), which traveled the same course as the *Indianapolis* and cruised through her wreckage. Bodies and debris were observed. Captain Sullivan stated: 'We had not received orders to zigzag. We had 4,000 troops on board. We had not been notified that an enemy submarine was in the area. The foregoing can be confirmed by referring to the official log of the USS *General R. L. Howze* for August of 1945.'

In a letter dated 10 February 1998, Dr. Lewis Haynes, the chief medical officer on board the *Indianapolis*, stated that, as he was treating Fleet Admiral Chester Nimitz at the Chelsea Naval Hospital, Admiral Nimitz told him that Captain McVay 'should not have been court-martialed.'" 10.

Ultimately, these discoveries for a simple history project became core pieces of evidence that passionately motivated young Hunter Scott to join with us to see the captain exonerated. His analysis eventually drew the attention of the *Indianapolis* survivors' organization, the media and Congressional Representative Joe Scarborough.

In 1998 Representative Scarborough introduced legislation

(H.R. 3610) seeking a presidential pardon for Captain McVay, not realizing that, in effect, Secretary Forrestal had already pardoned him in 1946 by remitting his sentence and restoring him to duty. In light of this, Representative Scarborough introduced a new resolution (H.J. Res. 48) when Congress convened in 1999. There he argued that Captain McVay's court-martial was morally unsustainable and that his conviction was a miscarriage of justice. Hunter Scott and fourteen *Indianapolis* survivors also testified before congress in support of the resolution. The hearing was so persuasive that Senator Bob Smith of New Hampshire introduced an identical companion measure in the Senate (S.J. Res. 23). The evidence was so compelling that sixteen senators joined Smith's resolution as co-sponsors and over one hundred House members joined as co-sponsors of the Scarborough resolution.

On September 14, 1999, Senator John Warner (R-VA), chairman of the Senate Armed Services Committee, agreed to hold a hearing to consider Senator Smith's joint resolution. Seventeen survivors submitted statements for the record and ten survivors appeared in person. Survivors Giles McCoy, Harlan Twible, and Paul Murphy (president of the survivor's organization), along with Dan Kurzman, author of *Fatal Voyage* were all witnesses on behalf of Senator Smith's resolution.

Thankfully, the legislation was passed by Congress and signed by President Clinton. The language concerning Captain McVay read:

Sense of Congress Concerning Charles Butler McVay III— With respect to the sinking of the USS *Indianapolis* (CA-35) on July 30, 1945, and the subsequent court-martial conviction of the ship's commanding officer, Captain Charles Butler McVay III, arising from that sinking, it is the sense of Congress:

(1) in light of the remission by the Secretary of Navy of the sentence of the court-martial and the restoration of Captain McVay to active duty by the Chief of Naval Operations, Fleet Admiral Chester Nimitz, that the American people should now recognize Captain McVay's lack of culpability for the tragic loss of the USS *Indianapolis* and the lives of the men who died as a result of the sinking of that vessel; and

(2) in light of the fact that certain exculpatory information was not available to the court-martial board and that Captain McVay's conviction resulted therefrom, that Captain McVay's military record should now reflect that he is exonerated for the loss of the

USS *Indianapolis* and so many of her crew. 11.

Every survivor with whom I have spoken joins with me in applauding the efforts of Hunter Scott and all the other senators, members of Congress and concerned citizens instrumental in securing justice for our captain, and resolution for the men that served him.

Epilogue

⚓

Blessed be the God and Father of our Lord Jesus Christ,
who according to His great mercy has caused us to be born again
to a living hope through the resurrection of Jesus Christ
from the dead,
to obtain an inheritance which is imperishable and undefiled
and will not fade away,
reserved in heaven for you, who are protected by the power of God
through faith for a salvation ready to be revealed in the last time.
In this you greatly rejoice,
even though now for a little while, if necessary,
you have been distressed by various trials,
that the proof of your faith,
being more precious than gold which is perishable,
even though tested by fire,
may be found to result in praise and glory and honor at the

revelation of Jesus Christ;

and though you have not seen Him, you love Him,

and though you do not see Him now,

but believe in Him,

you greatly rejoice with joy inexpressible and full of glory,

obtaining as the outcome of your faith the salvation of your souls.

1 Peter 1:3-9

Due to a combination of communication errors, military protocol, and scheduling bureaucracy, the navy had never sent a search party to look for us—even though we had not reached our destination on time. Although all of us experienced a great tragedy, I have never been sorry I joined the United States Navy. Nothing is too great to protect freedom for our country.

Survivor Dale F. Krueger

On August 2, 1995, the monument to the USS Indianapolis *(CA-35) was unveiled. A piece of the USS* Arizona *was placed inside the monument. The ships were the first and last American vessels to sink during the struggle for freedom. Building the monument was not only a proud moment for me and the other crewmembers; it was also an opportunity for me to come to grips with that tragic event that happened so long ago.*

Survivor James E. O'Donnell

I know that only death will bring peace to me by blocking my mind of these horrors. I sometimes think that my shipmates who were killed or eaten by sharks were the lucky ones. We who were left have had almost fifty years of mental pain. After 50 years, dates and faces lose their distinction, but the horror never goes away. I suffer long periods of depression and I cannot shake the feeling. The older I get the more it bothers me.

Survivor Cozell L. Smith Jr.

I am grateful to my Lord and Savior, Jesus Christ, for bringing me through this ordeal and giving me the strength and will power to put it behind me and go on with my life.

Survivor Lyle Umenhoffer

THERE REMAINS A SPECIAL BOND between the survivors and their families even to this day. The fiery crucible of our ordeal at sea has, for many, tempered the steel of our faith in God and forged a powerful sword of patriotism for the country we love. Every other year the survivors and their families and friends meet in July in Indianapolis, Indiana for a reunion—a wonderful season of fellowship, worship and memorial.

The USS *Indianapolis* (CA-35) Survivors Memorial Organization designed, erected and financed the USS *Indianapolis* (CA-35) National Memorial in honor of the ship and her crew, dedicated on August 2, 1995. It was designated a National Memorial by an act of Congress in 1995, one of only twenty-six such memorials. It is essentially a beautifully landscaped park open to the public twenty-four hours a day, seven days a week, located at the north end of the Canal Walk in Indianapolis, Indiana. A stately monument resembling the *Indianapolis* graces the site, with the names of the ship's company and one passenger who made up her final crew engraved on its south face.

Families, friends and supporters of the men of the *Indianapolis* have now formed an organization called The Second Watch dedicated to assist the USS *Indianapolis* Survivors Organization and to promote citizenship and patriotism in our beloved country. I applaud their efforts. We must continue to remind our children that freedom is not free. And for this reason, many brave men and women have sacrificed their lives for this great nation.

Due to the treacherous terrain and enormous depths in the Philippine Sea where the *Indy* was sunk, recent attempts to locate the ship have proven futile. After a grueling exploration was conducted, the crew of an expeditionary vessel named the *Sea Eagle* concluded that their disappointing search must be abandoned. Consequently, the passengers, explorers, and a few *Indy* survivors on board conducted a most appropriate and appreciated memorial service. An American flag presented to the *Indianapolis* survivors by Admiral Tom Fellin was draped over a makeshift raft. A simple block of granite was placed on the flag, along with a plaque commemorating the ship and her crew.

After a brief memorial service, the "memorial barge" was solemnly lowered into the water off the fantail of the ship to float in silent honor of the sacrifice that was once made in that place. After a few minutes, the crew tugged on the line to tip the raft, symbolically reenacting what happened on that tragic July night in 1945. Once again, a sacred cargo slipped into a watery grave. While I was not there, I can vividly see in my imagination the flag and the memorandums sinking into the final resting place of my shipmates. I hope that this act of honorable remembrance will bring comfort to the families who still mourn.

For me, the ordeal of the USS *Indianapolis* will never be over until the Lord takes me home to be with Him. My experiences on board the *Indy* and my anguish of soul while lost at sea remain stunning reminders of the sinfulness of man, the providence of God and His saving grace. For I know that by the grace of God I was not only saved out of the depths of the Pacific, but more amazingly, out of the depths of my sin. Therefore, my confident hope will always remain in Him, a sentiment shared by the inspired psalmist who said, "Out of the depths I have cried to Thee, O LORD. Lord, hear my voice! Let Thine ears be attentive to the voice of my supplications. If Thou, LORD, shouldst mark iniquities, O Lord, who could stand? But there is forgiveness with Thee, that Thou mayest be feared" (Psalm 130:1-4).

Occasionally someone will say to me, "So you were one of the lucky ones." While I appreciate their kind sentiment, I know in my heart that luck had nothing to do with our rescue. In fact, I am convinced that there is no such thing as luck. I refuse to even include the word in my vocabulary. Our world is not ruled by chance or fate, but by a sovereign God "who works all things after the counsel of His will" (Ephesians 1:11). His providential rule knows no bounds, nor does His omnipotence have limits. For God has said, "The One forming light and creating darkness, causing well-being and creating calamity; I am the LORD who does all these" (Isaiah 45:7).

From the beginning of our creation, God has ordered the events of history to ultimately glorify Himself through the person and work of His Son, the Lord Jesus Christ. For "there is salvation in no one else; for there is no other name under heaven that has been given among men, by which we must be saved" (Acts 4:12). Every life story either bears witness to His sovereign grace, or denies it. But no life has ever been lived apart from the purposes of God. He alone orchestrates the affairs of His creation. Like all the marvelous and mysterious doctrines of God, the co-existence of divine sovereignty and human responsibility remain an incomprehensible paradox to the human mind—certainly one that offends man's rabid commitment to self-determination. But as I look back over my life through the lens of Scripture, I have no doubt that indeed God is in control, and, without coercion, He uses human means to accomplish His purposes—even the sinking of the USS *Indianapolis*. I therefore find solace in the inscrutable mysteries of God and relax in the safety of His sovereign rule.

While I would never claim to know the mind of God, I do claim His promise that He "causes all things to work together for good to those who love God, to those who are called according to His purpose. For whom He foreknew, He also predestined to become conformed to the image of His Son, that He might be the first-born among many brethren; and whom He predestined, these He also called; and whom He called, these He also justified; and whom He justified, these He also glorified" (Romans 8:28-30). With these sacred truths resonating within my heart, I am at peace with what God allowed to happen. And I pray that my testimony to the praise of His glory will inspire many to humble themselves before the Lover of their souls in genuine repentance and place their faith in our Savior, the Lord Jesus Christ. To this end I salute my shipmates, their families and friends.

About USS *Indianapolis* Survivor Edgar Harrell

Edgar Harrell owned and operated the Pella Window Company, Inc., Rock Island, Illinois for thirty-five years until his retirement in 1985. During the years 1970 to 1985, he served on the board of trustees of the Moody Bible Institute, in Chicago, Illinois, and has been a popular Bible teacher and lay minister throughout his adult life. He has enjoyed many years of fishing and big game hunting in the Rocky Mountains from Alaska to New Mexico, and currently resides in Paris, Tennessee with his wife Ola, together enjoying their two children, eight grandchildren and four great-grandchildren. As a survivor of the USS *Indianapolis* (www.indysurvivor.com), Mr. Harrell speaks extensively around the United States about his experience at sea.

About the Author David Harrell

With a unique background as an avid hunter, horseman and musician, David Harrell first studied piano at the Moody Bible Institute until a finger injury caused him to shift his academic pursuits to Bible theology and biblical counseling. After attending the Moody Bible Institute, he graduated from Grace College, Grace Theological Seminary and the Oxford Graduate School where he earned the Doctor of Philosophy degree in Religion and Society. Dr. Harrell is a former associate professor of Biblical Counseling at the Master's College. His extensive wilderness expeditions, combined with a passion for Bible theology have made him a popular Bible expositor. He has been the pastor-teacher of Calvary Bible Church, Joelton, Tennessee, since July 1995 (www.cbctn.org). He is married to Nancy and together they have three children and four grandchildren.

The Navy Hymn

Eternal Father, strong to save,
Whose arm hath bound the restless wave,
Who bidd'st the mighty ocean deep
Its own appointed limits keep;
Oh, hear us when we cry to Thee,
For those in peril on the sea!

O Christ! Whose voice the waters heard
And hushed their raging at Thy word,
Who walked'st on the foaming deep,
And calm amidst its rage didst sleep;
Oh, hear us when we cry to Thee,
For those in peril on the sea!

Most Holy Spirit! Who didst brood

Upon the chaos dark and rude,

And bid its angry tumult cease,

And give, for wild confusion, peace;

Oh, hear us when we cry to Thee,

For those in peril on the sea!

O Trinity of love and power!

Our brethren shield in danger's hour;

From rock and tempest, fire and foe,

Protect them wheresoe'er they go;

Thus evermore shall rise to Thee

Glad hymns of praise from land and sea.

Alternate verse by J.E. Seim (1966)

Eternal Father, grant, we pray,

To all Marines, both night and day,

The courage, honor, strength, and skill

Their land to serve, thy law fulfill;

Be thou the shield forevermore

From every peril to the Corps.

The "Navy Hymn" is *Eternal Father, Strong to Save*. The original words were written as a poem in 1860 by William Whiting of Winchester, England, for a student who was about to sail for the

United States. The melody, published in 1861, was composed by fellow Englishman, Re. John Bacchus Dykes, an Episcopalian clergyman.

The hymn, found in most hymnals, is known as the "Navy Hymn" because it is sung at the U.S. Naval Academy in Annapolis, Maryland. It is also sung on ships of the Royal Navy (U.K.) and has been translated into French.

Eternal Father was the favorite hymn of President Franklin Delano Roosevelt and was sung at his funeral in Hyde Park, New York, in April 1945. It was also played by the Navy Band in 1963 as President John F. Kennedy's body was carried up the steps of the U.S. Capitol to lie in state. Roosevelt had served as Secretary of the Navy and Kennedy was a PT boat commander in World War II.

Information from *The Presbyterian Hymnal Companion* by LindaJo H. McKim, Westminister/John Knox Press, Louisville, Ky. 1993.

The Marine Corps Hymn

From the halls of Montezuma
To the shores of Tripoli,
We fight our country's battles
In the air, on land, and sea.

First to fight for right and freedom,
And to keep our honor clean,
We are proud to claim the title
Of United States Marine.

Our flags unfurl'd to every breeze
From dawn to setting sun;
We have fought in every clime and place
Where we could take a gun.

In the snow of far-off northern lands
And in sunny tropic scenes,
You will find us always on the job –
The United States Marines.

Here's health to you and to our Corps
Which we are proud to serve;
In many a strife we've fought for life
And never lost our nerve.

If the Army and the Navy
Ever look on Heaven's scenes,
They will find the streets are guarded
By United States Marines.

NOTES

CHAPTER 1

1. Hashimoto, Mochitsura. *Sunk!: The Story of the Japanese Submarine Fleet, 1942-1945.* (New York: Henry Holt, 1954), 57.
2. Finneran, Patrick J. *A Short History of the USS Indianapolis,* The USS *Indianapolis* (CA-35) Survivors Organization, **www.ussindianapolis.org.**
3. Ibid.
4. Brady, Daniel E., of the V (Aviation) Division, personal account recounted in Patrick J. Finneran's article, *"The Tragedy of the USS Indianapolis (CA-35)",* 1994.

CHAPTER 2

1. Moore, Katherine D., *Good-bye, Indy Maru,* (Knoxville, TN: Lori Publications, 1991), 52.

2. Dictionary of American Fighting Ships, Vol. III, 1968, Navy Department, Office of the Chief of Naval Operations, Naval History Division, Washington, D.C., 434.

3. Ibid., 435

4. Ibid., 435

5. Ibid., 435

6. Ibid., 435

7. Ibid., 435

8. Stanton, Doug, *In Harm's Way*, (Henry Holt and Company, New York, 2001), 37.

9. Finneran, Patrick J. *A Short History of the USS Indianapolis*, The USS *Indianapolis* (CA-35) Survivors Organization, www.ussindianapolis.org.

CHAPTER 3

1. Stanton, Doug, *In Harm's Way*, (Henry Holt and Company, New York, 2001), 73-74.

2. Ibid., 75

3. Ibid., 78

4. Ibid., 77

5. Lech, Raymond B. *All the Drowned Sailers.* (New York: Stein and Day, 1982), 31.

6. Newcomb, Richard F. *Abandon Ship!: Death of the USS Indianapolis,* Bloomington: (Indiana University Press, 1958), 57.

7. Hashimoto, Mochitsura. *Sunk!: The Story of the Japanese Submarine Fleet, 1942-1945.* (New York: Henry Holt, 1954), 172.

8. Newcomb, Richard F. *Abandon Ship!: Death of the USS Indianapolis,* Bloomington: (Indiana University Press, 1958), 8.

9. Hashimoto, Mochitsura. *Sunk!: The Story of the Japanese Submarine Fleet, 1942-1945.* (New York: Henry Holt, 1954), 177.

10. Stanton, Doug, *In Harm's Way,* (Henry Holt and Company, New York, 2001), 80.

11. Newcomb, Richard F. *Abandon Ship!: Death of the USS Indianapolis,* Bloomington: (Indiana University Press, 1958), 8.

12. Hashimoto, Mochitsura. *Sunk!: The Story of the Japanese Submarine Fleet, 1942-1945.* (New York: Henry Holt, 1954), 220.

13. Ibid., 221-225.

CHAPTER 4

1. Stanton, Doug, *In Harm's Way*, (Henry Holt and Company, New York, 2001), 172.
2. Ibid., 180-182

CHAPTER 6

1. Wren, L. Peter, *We Were There: The USS Indianapolis Tragedy*, (L. Peter Wren, Richmond, Virginia, 2002), 11.
2. Stanton, Doug, *In Harm's Way*, (Henry Holt and Company, New York, 2001), 216.
3. Ibid., 211-216
4. Ibid., 219
5. Ibid., 225
6. Ibid., 225-226
7. Marks, Adrian. *Selected Speeches of R. Adrian Marks*, (1990), 32.
8. Ibid., 34
9. Ibid., 36-39
10. Ibid., 39-41
11. Ibid., 25-30

CHAPTER 7

1. Stanton, Doug, *In Harm's Way*, (Henry Holt and Company, New York, 2001), 239.

2. Wren, L. Peter. *Those In Peril on the Sea*. (Richmond, VA: L. Peter Wren, 1999), 162.

3. Stanton, Doug, *In Harm's Way*, (Henry Holt and Company, New York, 2001), 239.

4. Ibid., 253

5. *The Paris Intelligence,* March 16, 1994.

6. Marks, Adrian. *Selected Speeches of R. Adrian Marks*, (1990), 53.

7. Ibid., 45-46

8. Ibid., 44

CHAPTER 8

1. Prepared Statement by Dr. Giles G. McCoy: Hearing before the Committee on Armed Services United States Senate One Hundred Sixth Congress, First Session, September 14, 1999. Washington: (U.S. Government Printing Office, 2000), 13.

2. Kurzman, Dan. *Fatal Voyage: The Sinking of the USS Indianapolis*. New York: (Atheneum, 1990), 202.

3. Ibid., 204-206

4. *The Sinking of USS Indianapolis*: Navy Department Press Release Charges and Specifications in Case of Capt. Charles B. McVay, III, USN, 3 Dec. 1945

5. Ibid.

6. Newcomb, Richard F. *Abandon Ship!: Death of the USS Indianapolis*, (Bloomington: Indiana University Press, 1958), 252.

7. Kurzman, Dan. *Fatal Voyage: The Sinking of the USS Indianapolis*. New York: (Atheneum, 1990), 212-213.

8. Newcomb, Richard F. *Abandon Ship!: Death of the USS Indianapolis*, (Bloomington: Indiana University Press 1958), 252.

9. Scott, Hunter. *Timeline to Justice,* Naval History Magazine, July-August 1998.

10. Ibid.

11. *Language of the Legislation, The USS Indianapolis (CA-35) Survivors Organization*, www.ussindianapolis.org.

OTHER RESOURCES

⚓

Saved By a Substitute

In his twelve page booklet, former Navy petty officer O. Talmadge Spence describes a fascinating account of how "the merciful providence of God" prevented him from boarding the doomed USS *Indianapolis* by only two hours and ultimately led him to a saving faith in the Lord Jesus Christ. Dr. Spence later became the founder and President of Foundations Bible College, Dunn, North Carolina. A copy of this booklet can be obtained by contacting Foundations Bible College, P.O. Box 1166, Dunn, NC 28335 800-849-8761; **www.foundations.edu**.

ONLY 317 SURVIVED!

ONLY 317 SURVIVED! is a fascinating book of personal testimonies written by 102 survivors of the USS *Indianapolis* and forty deceased survivor's families. Each personal recollection reminds the reader of the triumph of courage and the enormous sacrifice that was made for our freedom. For more information, contact **www.ussindianapolis.org**.

The Final Crew
of the USS *Indianapolis* (CA-35)

CREW AND OFFICERS

ABBOTT, George S., S1
ACOSTA, Charles M., MM3
ADAMS, Leo H., S1 *
ADAMS, Pat L., S2
ADORANTE, Dante W., S2
AKINES, William R., S2 *
ALBRIGHT, Charles E. Jr., COX
ALLARD, Vincent J., QM3 *
ALLEN, Paul F., S1
ALLMARAS, Harold D., F2
ALTSCHULER, Allan H., S2 *
ALVEY, Edward W. Jr., AerM2
AMICK, Homer I., S2
ANDERSEN, Lawrence J., SK2
ANDERSON, Erick T., S2 *
ANDERSON, Leonard O., MM3
ANDERSON, Richard L., F2
ANDERSON, Sam G., S2
ANDERSON, Vincent U., BM1
ANDREWS, William R., S2 *
ANNIS, James B. Jr., CEMA
ANTHONY, Harold R., PHM3
ANTONIE, Charles J., F2
ANUNTI, John M., M2 *
ARMENTA, Lorenzo, SC2
ARMISTEAD, John H., S2 *
ARNOLD, Carl L., AMM3
ASHFORD, Chester W., WT2
ASHFORD, John T. Jr., RT3 *
ATKINSON, J. P., COX
AULL, Joseph H., S2
AULT, William F., S2 *
AYOTTE, Lester J., S2
BACKUS, Thomas H., LT (jg)
BAKER, Daniel A., S2
BAKER, Frederick H., S2
BAKER, William M. Jr., EM1
BALDRIDGE, Clovis R., EM2 *
BALL, Emmet E., S2
BALLARD, Courtney J., SSM3
BARENTHIN, Leonard W., S2
BARKER, Robert C. Jr., RT1
BARKSDALE, Thomas L., FC3
BARNES, Paul C., F2
BARNES, Willard M., MM1
BARRA, Raymond J., CGMA
BARRETT, James B., S2
BARRY, Charles, LT (jg)
BARTO, Lloyd P., S1 *

BARTON, George S., Y3
BATEMAN, Bernard B., F2 *
BATENHORST, Wilfred J., MM3
BATSON, Eugene C., S2
BATTEN, Robert E., S1
BATTS, Edward D., STM1
BEANE, James A., F2 *
BEATY, Donald L., S1 *
BECKER, Myron M., WT2
BEDDINGTON, Charles E., S1
BEDSTED, Leo A. K., F1
BEISTER, Richard J., WT3
BELCHER, James R., S1 *
BELL, Maurice G., S1 *
BENNETT, Dean R., HA1
BENNETT, Ernest F., B3
BENNETT, Toney W., ST3
BENNING, Harry, S1
BENTON, Clarence U., CFCP *
BERNACIL, Concepcion P., FC3 *
BERRY, Joseph, Jr., STM1
BERRY, William H., ST3
BEUKEMA, Kenneth J., S2
BEUSCHLEIN, Joseph C., S2
BIDDISON, Charles L., S1
BILLINGS, Robert B., ENS
BILLINGSLEY, Robert F., GM3
BILZ, Robert E., S2
BISHOP, Arthur Jr., S2
BITONTI, Louis P., S1 *
BLACKWELL, Fermon M., SSML3
BLANTHORN, Bryan, S1 *
BLUM, Donald J., ENS *
BOEGE, Raymond R., S2
BOGAN, Jack R., RM1
BOLLINGER, Richard H., S1
BOOTH, Sherman C., S1 *
BORTON, Herbert E., SC2
BOSS, Norbert G., S2
BOTT, Wilbur M., S2
BOWLES, Eldridge W., S1
BOWMAN, Charles E., CTC
BOYD, Troy H., GM3
BRADLEY, William H., S2
BRAKE, John Jr., S2
BRANDT, Russell L., F2 *
BRAUN, Neal F., S2
BRAY, Harold J. Jr., S2 *
BRICE, R. V., S2
BRIDGE, Wayne A., S2

BRIGHT, Chester L., S2
BRILEY, Harold V., MAM3
BROOKS, Ulysess R., CWTA
BROPHY, Thomas D'Arcy Jr., ENS
BROWN, Edward A., WT3
BROWN, Edward J., S1 *
BRUCE, Russell W., S2
BRULE, Maurice J., S2
BRUNDIGE, Robert H., S1 *
BRUNEAU, Charles A., GM3
BUCKETT, Victor R., Y2 *
BUDISH, David, S2
BULLARD, John K., S1 *
BUNAI, Robert P., SM1 *
BUNN, Horace G, S2
BURDORF, Wilbert J., COX *
BURKHARTSMEIER, Anton T., S1
BURKHOLTZ, Frank Jr., EM3
BURLESON, Martin L., S1
BURRS, John W., S1
BURT, William George A., QM3
BURTON, Curtis H., S1 *
BUSHONG, John R., GM3
CADWALLADER, John J., RT3
CAIN, Alfred B., RT3
CAIRO, William G., BUG1
CALL, James E., RM3
CAMERON, John W., GM2
CAMP, Garrison, STM2
CAMPANA, Paul, RDM3
CAMPBELL, Hamer E. Jr., GM3 *
CAMPBELL, Louis D., AOM3 *
CAMPBELL, Wayland D., SF3
CANDALINO, Paul L., LT (jg)
CANTRELL, Billy G, F2
CARNELL, Lois W., S2
CARPENTER, Willard A., SM3
CARR, Harry L., S2
CARROLL, Gregory K., S1
CARROLL, Rachel W., COX
CARSON, Clifford, F1
CARSTENSEN, Richard, S2
CARTER, Grover C., S1 *
CARTER, Lindsey L., S2 *
CARTER, Lloyd G, COX *
CARVER, Grover C., S1 *
CASSIDY, John C., S1 *
CASTALDO, Patrick P., GM2
CASTIAUX, Ray V., S2
CASTO, William H., S1
CAVIL, Robert R., MM2
CAVITT, Clinton J., WT3
CELAYA, Adolfo V., F2 *
CENTAZZO, Frank J., SM3 *
CHAMNESS, John D., S2 *
CHANDLER, Lloyd N., S2

CHART, Joseph, EM3
CHRISTIAN, Lewis E. Jr., WO
CLARK, Eugene, CK3
CLARK, Orsen N., S2 *
CLEMENTS, Harold P., S2
CLINTON, George W., S1 *
CLINTON, Leland J., LT (jg)
COBB, William L., MOMM3
COLE, Walter H., CRMA
COLEMAN, Cedric F., LCDR
COLEMAN, Robert E., F2 *
COLLIER, Charles R., RM2 *
COLLINS, James, STM1
COLVIN, Frankie L., SSMT2
CONDON, Barna T., RDM1
CONNELLY, David F., ENS
CONRAD, James P., EM3
CONSER, Donald L., SC2
CONSIGLIO, Joseph W., FC2
CONWAY, Thomas M., Rev., LT
COOK, Floyd E., SF3
COOPER, Dale, Jr., F2
COPELAND, Willard J., S2
COSTNER, Homer J., COX *
COUNTRYMAN, Robert E., S2
COWEN, Donald R., FC3 *
COX, Alford E., GM3
COX, Loel Dene, S2 *
CRABB, Donald C., RM2
CRANE, Granville S. Jr., MM2 *
CREWS, Hugh C., LT (jg)
CRITES, Orval D., WT1
CROUCH, Edwin M., CAPT (Passenger)
CRUM, Charles J., S2
CRUZ, Jose S., CCKA
CURTIS, Erwin E., CTCP
DAGENBART, Charles R. Jr., PHM2
DALE, Elwood R., F1
DANIEL, Harold W., CBMA *
DANIELLO, Anthony G., S1
DAVIS, James C., RM3
DAVIS, Kenneth G, F1
DAVIS, Stanley G., LT (jg)
DAVIS, Thomas E., SM2
DAY, Richard R. Jr., S2
DEAN, John T. Jr., S2
DeBERNARDI, Louie, BM1 *
DeFOOR, Walton, RDM3
DeMARS, Edgar J., CBMA
DeMENT, Dayle P., S1
DENNEY, Lloyd Jr., S2
DEWING, Ralph O., FC3 *
DIMOND, John N., S2
DIZELSKE, William B., MM2 *
DOLLINS, Paul, RM2
DONALD, Lyle H., EM1

DONEY, William Jr., F2
DONNER, Clarence W., RT3 *
DORMAN, William B., S1
DORNETTO, Frank P., WT1
DOSS, James M., S2
DOUCETT, Roland O., S2
DOUGLAS, Gene D., F2*
DOVE, Bassil R., SKD2
DOWDY, Lowell S., CWO
DRANE, James A., GM3
DRAYTON, William H., EM2 *
DRISCOLL, David L., LT (jg)
DRONET, Joseph E. J., S2 *
DRUMMOND, James J., F2
DRURY, Richard E., S2
DRYDEN, William H., MM1 *
DUFRAINE, Delbert E., S1
DUNBAR, Jess L., F2
DURAND, Ralph J. Jr., S2
DYCUS, Donald, S2
EAKINS, Morris B., F2
EAMES, Paul H. Jr., ENS
EASTMAN, Chester S., S2
ECK, Harold A., S2 *
EDDINGER, John W., S1
EDDY, Richard L., RM3
EDWARDS, Alwyn C., F2
EDWARDS, Roland J., BM1
E'GOLF, Harold W., S2
ELLIOTT, Harry W., S2
ELLIOTT, Kenneth A., S1
EMERY, William F., S1
EMSLEY, William J., S1
ENGELSMAN, Ralph, S2
EPPERSON, Ewell, S2
EPPERSON, George L., S1
ERICKSON, Theodore M., S2 *
ERNST, Robert C., F2
ERWIN, Louis H., COX *
ETHIER, Eugene E., EM3 *
EUBANKS, James H., S1
EVANS, Arthur J., PHM2
EVANS, Claudus, GM3 *
EVERETT, Charles N., EM2
EVERS, Lawrence L., CMMA
EYET. Donald A., S1
FANTASIA, Frank A., F2
FARBER, Sheldon L., S2
FARLEY, James W., S1
FARMER, Archie C., COX *
FARRIS, Eugene F., S1 *
FAST HORSE, Vincent, S2
FEAKES, Fred A., AOM1 *
FEDORSKI, Nicholas W., S1 *
FEENEY, Paul R., S2
FELTS, Donald J., BM1 *

FERGUSON, Albert E., CMMA *
FERGUSON, Russell M., RT3
FIGGINS, Harley D., WT2
FIRESTONE, Kenneth F., FC2
FIRMIN, John A. H., S2
FITTING, Johnny W., GM1 *
FLATEN, Harold J., WT2 *
FLEISCHAUER, Donald W., S1
FLESHMAN, Vern L., S2
FLYNN, James M. Jr., S1
FLYNN, Joseph A., CDR
FOELL, Cecil D., ENS
FORTIN, Verlin L., WT3 *
FOSTER, Verne E., F2 *
FOX, William H. Jr., F2 *
FRANCOIS, Norbert E., F1 *
FRANK, Rudolph A., S2
FRANKLIN, Jack R., RDM3
FREEZE, Howard B., LT (jg)
FRENCH, Douglas O., FC3
FRENCH, Jimmy Jr., QM3
FRITZ, Leonard A., MM3
FRONTINO, Vincent F., MOMM3
FRORATH, Donald H., S2
FUCHS, Herman F., CWO
FULLER, Arnold A., F2
FULTON, William C., CRMA
FUNKHOUSER, Robert M., ART2 *
GABRILLO, Juan, S2 *
GAITHER, Forest M., FC2
GALANTE, Angelo, S2 *
GALBRAITH, Norman S., MM2 *
GARDNER, Roscoe W., F2 *
GARDNER, Russell T., F2
GARNER, Glenn R., MM2
GAUSE, Robert P., QM1 *
GAUSE, Rubin C. Jr., ENS
GEMZA, Rudolph A., FC3 *
GEORGE, Gabriel V., MM3 *
GERNGROSS, Frederick J. Jr., ENS
GETTLEMAN, Robert A., S2 *
GIBSON, Buck W., GM3 *
GIBSON, Curtis W., S2
GIBSON, Ganola F., MM3
GILBERT, Warner Jr. S1
GILCREASE, James, S2 *
GILL, Paul E., WT2
GILMORE, Wilbur A., S2
GISMONDI, Michael V., S1
GLADD, Millard, Jr., MM2 *
GLAUB, Francis A., GM2
GLENN, Jay R., AMM3 *
GLOVKA, Erwin S., S2
GODFREY, Marlo R., RM3
GOECKEL, Ernest S., LT (jg)
GOFF, Thomas G., SF3 *

GOLDEN, Curry., STM1
GOLDEN, James L., S1
GONZALES, Ray A., S2
GOOCH, William L., F2 *
GOOD, Robert K., MM3
GOODWIN, Oliver A., CRTA
GORE, Leonard F., S2
GORECKI, Joseph W., SK3
GOTTMAN, Paul J., S2
GOVE, Carroll L., S2
GRAY, Willis L., S1 *
GREATHOUSE, Bud R., S1
GREEN, Robert U., S2
GREEN, Tolbert Jr., S1 *
GREENE, Samuel G., S1
GREENLEE, Charles I., S2 *
GREER, Bob E., S2
GREGORY, Garland G., F1
GREIF, Matthias D., WT3
GRIES, Richard C., F2
GRIEST, Frank D., GM3
GRIFFIN, Jackie D., S1
GRIFFITH, Robert S., S1 *
GRIFFITHS, Leonard S., S2
GRIGGS, Donald R., F1
GRIMES, David E., S2
GRIMES, James F., S2
GROCE, Floyd V., RDM2
GROCH, John T., MM3
GUENTHER, Morgan E., EM3
GUERRERO, John G., S1
GUILLOT, Murphy U., F1
GUYE, Ralph L. Jr., QM3
GUYON, Harold L., F1
HABERMAN, Bernard, S2
HADUCH, John M., S1
HALE, Robert B., LT
HALE, William F., S2
HALL, Pressie, F1
HALLORAN, Edward G., MM3
HAM, Saul A., S1
HAMBO, William P., PHM3
HAMMEN, Robert, PHOM3
HAMRICK, James J., S2
HANCOCK, William A., GM3
HANKINSON, Clarence W., F2
HANSEN, Henry, S2
HANSON, Harley C., WO *
HARLAND, George A., S2
HARP, Charlie H., S1
HARPER, Vasco, STM1
HARRIS, James D., F2
HARRIS, Willard E., F2
HARRISON, Cecil M., CWO*
HARRISON, Frederick E., S2
HARRISON, James M., S1

HART, Fred Jr., RT2 *
HARTRICK, Willis B., MM1
HATFIELD, Willie N., S2 *
HAUBRICH, Cloud D., S2
HAUSER, Jack I., SK2
HAVENER, Harlan C., F2*
HAVINS, Otha A., Y3 *
HAYES, Charles D., LCDR
HAYLES, Felix, CK3
HAYNES, Lewis L., MC, LCDR*
HAYNES, Robert A., LT
HAYNES, William A., S1
HEERDT, Raymond E., F2
HEGGIE, William A., RDM3
HEINZ, Richard A., HA1
HELLER, John, S2 *
HELLER, Robert J. Jr., S2
HELSCHER, Ralph J., S1
HELT, Jack E., F2
HENDERSON, Ralph L., S1
HENDRON, James R. Jr., F2
HENRY, Earl O., DC, LCDR
HENSCH, Erwin F., LT *
HENSLEY, Clifford, SSMB2
HERBERT, Jack E., BM1
HERNDON, Duane, S2
HERSHBERGER, Clarence L., S1 *
HERSTINE, James F., ENS
HICKEY, Harry T., RM3
HICKS, Clarence, S1
HIEBERT, Lloyd H., GM1
HILL, Clarence M., CWTP
HILL, Joe W., STM1
Hill, Nelson P. Jr., LT
HILL, Richard N., ENS
HIND, Lyle L., S2 *
HINES, Lionel G., WT1
HINKEN, John R. Jr., F2*
HOBBS, Melvin D., S1
HODGE, Howard H., RM2 *
HODGINS, Lester B., S2
HODSHIRE, John W., S2
HOERRES, George J., S2
HOLDEN, Punciano A., ST1
HOLLINGSWORTH, Jimmie L., STM2
HOLLOWAY, Andrew J., S2
HOLLOWAY, Ralph H., COX
HOOGERWERF, John Jr., F1
HOOPER, Roy L., AMM1
HOOPES, Gordon H., S2 *
HOPPER, Prentice W., S1
HORNER, Durward R., WO *
HORR, Wesley A., F2
HORRIGAN, John G., F1
HORVATH, George J., F1 *
HOSKINS, William O., Y3 *

HOUCK, Richard E., EM3 *
HOUSTON, Robert G., Fl.
HOUSTON, William H., PHM2
HOV, Donald A., Sl
HOWISON, John D., ENS *
HUBELI, Joseph F., S2 *
HUEBNER, Harry J., S1
HUGHES, Lawrence E., F2
HUGHES, Robert A., FC3
HUGHES, William E., SSML2
HUMPHREY, Maynard L., S2
HUNTER, Arthur R. Jr., QM1
HUNTLEY, Virgil C., CWO
HUPKA, Clarence E., BKR1 *
HURLEY, Woodrow, GM2 *
HURST, Robert H., LT
HURT, James E., S2
HUTCHISON, Merle B., S2
IGOU, Floyd Jr., RM2
IZOR, Walter E., Fl
JACKSON, Henry, STML
JACQUEMOT, Joseph A., S2 *
JADLOSKI, George K., S2
JAKUBISIN, Joseph S., S2
JAMES, Woodie E., COX *
JANNEY, Johns Hopkins, CDR
JARVIS, James K., AM3 *
JEFFERS, Wallace M., COX
JENNEY, Charles I., LT
JENSEN, Chris A., S2
JENSEN, Eugene W., S2 *
JEWELL, Floyd R., SK1
JOHNSON, Bernard J., S2
JOHNSON, Elwood W., S2
JOHNSON, George G., S2
JOHNSON, Harold B., S1
JOHNSON, Sidney B., Sl
JOHNSON, Walter M. Jr., Sl
JOHNSON, William A., Sl *
JOHNSTON, Earl R., BM2
JOHNSTON, Lewis E., Sl
JOHNSTON, Ray F., MM1
JOHNSTON, Scott A., F2
JONES, Clinton L., COX *
JONES, George E., S2
JONES, Jim, S2
JONES, Kenneth M., Fl MoMM
JONES, Sidney, Sl *
JONES, Stanley F., S2
JORDAN, Henry, STM2
JORDON, Thomas H., S2
JOSEY, Clifford O., S2
JUMP, David A., ENS
JURGENSMEYER, Alfred J., S2
JURKIEWICZ, Raymond S., Sl *
JUSTICE, Robert E., S2 *

KARPEL, Dan L., BM1
KARTER, Leo C. Jr., S2
KASTEN, Stanley O., HAl
KAWA, Raymond P., SK3
KAY, Gust C., Sl *
KAZMIERSKI, Walter, Sl *
KEENEY, Robert A., ENS
KEES, Shalous E., EM2 *
KEITH, Everette E., EM2
KELLY, Albert R., S2
KEMP, David P. Jr., SC3 *
KENLY, Oliver W., RDM3 *
KENNEDY, Andrew J. Jr., S2
KENNEDY, Robert A., Sl
KENNY, Francis J. P., S2
KEPHART, Paul, Sl
KERBY, Deo E., Sl *
KERN, Harry G., Sl
KEY, S. T., EM2
KEYES, Edward H., COX *
KIGHT, Audy C., Sl
KILGORE, Archie C., F2
KILLMAN, Robert E., GM3
KINARD, Nolan D., Sl
KINCAID, Joseph E., FC2
KING, A. C., Sl*
KING, Clarence Jr., STM2
KING, James T., Sl
KING, Richard E., S2
KING, Robert H., S2
KINNAMAN, Robert L., S2
KINZLE, Raymond A., BKR2 *
KIRBY, Harry, Sl
KIRK, James R., SC3
KIRKLAND, Marvin F., Sl*
KIRKMAN, Walter W., SF1
KISELICA, Joseph F., AMM2 *
KITTOE, James W., F2 *
KLAPPA, Ralph D., S2 *
KLAUS, Joseph F., Sl *
KLEIN, Raymond J., Sl
KLEIN, Theil J., SK3
KNERNSCHIELD, Andrew N., Sl
KNOLL, Paul E., COX
KNOTT, Elbern L., Sl
KNUDTSON, Raymond A., Sl
KNUPKE, Richard R., MM3
KOCH, Edward C., EM3 *
KOEGLER, Albert, Sl
KOEGLER, William, SC3
KOLAKOWSKI, Ceslaus, SM3
KOLLINGER, Robert E., Sl
KONESNY, John M., Sl
KOOPMAN, Walter F., F2
KOPPANG, Raymond L., LT (jg)
KOUSKI, Fred, GM3

KOVALICK, George R., S2
KOZIARA, George, S2 *
KOZIK, Raymond., S1
KRAWITZ, Henry J., MM3
KREIS, Clifford E., S1 *
KRON, Herman E. Jr., GM3
KRONENBERGER, William, M., GM3
KRUEGER, Dale F., F2 *
KRUEGER, Norman F., S2 *
KRUSE, Darwin G., S2
KRZYZEWSKI, John M., S2
KUHN, Clair J., S1
KULOVITZ, Raymond J., S2
KURLICH, George R., FC3 *
KURYLA, Michael N. Jr., COX *
KUSIAK, Alfred M., S2
KWIATKOWSKI, Marion J., S2
LABUDA, Arthur A., QM3
LaFONTAINE, Paul S., S1
LAKATOS, Emil J., MM3
LAKE, Murl C., S1
LAMB, Robert C., EM3
LAMBERT, Leonard F., S1
LANDON, William W. Jr., FC2
LANE, Ralph, CMMA*
LANTER, Kenley M., S1 *
LaPAGLIA, Carlos, GM2 *
LaPARL, Lawrence E. Jr., S2
LAPCZYNSKI, Edward W., S1
LARSEN, Melvin R., S2
LATIGUE, Jackson, STM1
LATIMER, Billy F., S1
LATZER, Solomon, S2
LAUGHLIN, Fain H., SK3
LAWS, George E., S1 *
LEATHERS, Williams B., MM3
LeBARON, Robert W., S2
LeBOW, Cleatus A., FC3 *
LEENERMAN, Arthur L., RDM3 *
LELUIKA, Paul P., S2
LESTINA, Francis J., S1
LETIZIA, Vincencio, S2
LETZ, Wilbert J., SK1
LeVALLEY, William D., EM2
LEVENTON, Mervin C., MM2
LeVIEUX, John J., F2
LEWELLEN, Thomas E., S2
LEWIS, James R., F2
LEWIS, John R., GM3
LINDEN, Charles G., WT2
LINDSAY, Norman L., SF3
LINK, George C., S1
LINN, Roy, S1
LINVILLE, Cecil H., SF2
LINVILLE, Harry J., S1
LIPPERT, Robert G., S1

LIPSKI, Stanley W., CDR
LITTLE, Frank E., MM2
LIVERMORE, Raymond I., S2
LOCH, Edwin P., S1
LOCKWOOD, Thomas H., S2 *
LOEFFLER, Paul E. Jr., S2
LOFTIS, James B. Jr., S1 *
LOFTUS, Ralph D., F2
LOHR, Leo W., S1
LOMBARDI, Ralph, S1
LONG, Joseph W., S1
LONGWELL, Donald J., S1
LOPEZ, Daniel B., F2 *
LOPEZ, Sam, S1 *
LORENC, Edward R., S2
LOYD, John F., WT2
LUCAS, Robert A., S2 *
LUCCA, Frank J., F2 *
LUHMAN, Emerson D., MM3
LUNDGREN, Albert D., S1
LUTTRULL, Claud A., COX
LUTZ, Charles H., S1
MAAS, Melvin A., S1 *
MABEE, Kenneth C., F2
MACE, Harold A., S2 *
MacFARLAND, Keith I., LT (jg)
MACHADO, Clarence J., WT2
MACK, Donald F., BUG1 *
MADAY, Antony F., AMM1 *
MADIGAN, Harry F., BM2
MAGDICS, Steve Jr., F2
MAGRAY, Dwain F., S2
MAKAROFF, Chester J., GM3 *
MAKOWSKI, Robert T., CWTA
MALDONADO, Salvador, BKR3 *
MALENA, Joseph J. Jr., GM2 *
MALONE, Cecil E., S2
MALONE, Elvin C., S1
MALONE, Michael L. Jr., LT (jg)
MALSKI, Joseph J., S1 *
MANESS, Charles F., F2
MANKIN, Howard J., GM3
MANN, Clifford E., S1
MANSKER, LaVoice, S2
MANTZ, Keith H., S1
MARCIULAITIS, Charles, S1
MARKMANN, Frederick H., WT1
MARPLE, Paul T., ENS
MARSHALL, John L., WT2
MARSHALL, Robert W., S2
MARTIN, Albert, S2
MARTIN, Everett G., S1
MASSIER, George A., S1
MASTRECOLA, Michael M., S2
MATHESON, Richard R., PHM3
MATRULLA, John, S1 *

MAUNTEL, Paul J., S2
MAXWELL, Farrell J., S1 *
McBRIDE, Ronald G., S1
McBRYDE, Frank E., S2
McCALL, Donald C., S2 *
McCLAIN, Raymond B., BM2 *
McCLARY, Lester E., S2
McCLURE, David L., EM2
McCOMB, Everett A., F1
McCORD, Edward Franklin Jr., EM3
McCORKLE, Ray R., S1
McCORMICK, Earl W., MOMM2
McCOSKEY, Paul F., S1
McCOY, John S. Jr., M2
McCRORY, Millard V. Jr., WT2 *
McDANIEL, Johnny A., S1
McDONALD, Franklin G. Jr., F2
McDONNER, David P. Jr., F1
McDOWELL, Robert E., S1
McELROY, Clarence E., S1 *
McFALL, Walter E., S2 *
McFEE, Carl S., SC1
McGINNIS, Paul W., SM3 *
McGINTY, John M., S1
McGUIGGAN, Robert M., S1 *
McGUIRE, Denis, S2
McGUIRK, Philip A., LT (jg)
McHENRY, Loren C. Jr., S1 *
McHONE, Ollie, F1
McKEE, George E. Jr., S1
McKENNA, Michael J., S1
McKENZIE, Ernest E., S1 *
McKINNON, Francis M., Y3
McKISSICK, Charles B., LT (jg) *
McKLIN, Henry T., S1 *
McLAIN, Patrick J., S2 *
McLEAN, Douglas B., EM3
McNABB, Thomas Jr., F2
McNICKLE, Arthur S., F1
McQUITTY, Roy E., COX
McVAY, Charles Butler III, CAPT *
McVAY, Richard C., Y3 *
MEADE, Sidney H., S1
MEHLBAUM, Raymond A., S1
MEIER, Harold E., S2
MELICHAR, Charles H., EM3
MELVIN, Carl L., F1
MENCHEFF Manual A., S2
MEREDITH, Charles E., S1 *
MERGLER, Charles M., RDM2
MESTAS, Nestor A., WT2 *
METCALF, David W., GM3
MEYER, Charles T., S2 *
MICHAEL, Bertrand F., BKR3
MICHAEL, Elmer O., S1
MICHNO, Arthur R., S2

MIKESKA, Willie W., S2
MIKOLAYEK, Joseph, COX *
MILBRODT, Glen L., S2 *
MILES, Theodore K., LT
MILLER, Artie R., GM2
MILLER, George E., F1
MILLER, Glenn E., S2
MILLER, Samuel George Jr., FC3
MILLER, Walter R., S2
MILLER, Walter W., B1
MILLER, Wilbur H., CMM
MILLS, William H., EM3
MINER, Herbert J. II, RT2 *
MINOR, Richard L., S1
MINOR, Robert W., S2
MIRES, Carl E., S2
MIRICH, Wally M., S1
MISKOWIEC, Theodore F., S1
MITCHELL, James E., S2 *
MITCHELL, James H. Jr., SK1
MITCHELL, Kenneth E., S1 *
MITCHELL, Norval Jerry Jr., S1 *
MITCHELL, Paul B., FC3
MITCHELL, Winston C., S1
MITTLER, Peter John Jr., GM3
MIXON, Malcom L., GM2
MLADY, Clarence C., S1 *
MODESITT, Carl E., S2 *
MODISHER, Melvin W., MC, LT (jg) *
MONCRIEF, Mack D., S2
MONKS, Robert B., GM3
MONTOYA, Frank E., S1
MOORE, Donald G., S2
MOORE, Elbert, S2
MOORE, Harley E., S1
MOORE, Kyle C., LCDR
MOORE, Wyatt P., BKR1
MORAN, Joseph J., RM1 *
MORGAN, Eugene S., BM2 *
MORGAN, Glenn G., BGM3 *
MORGAN, Lewis E., S2
MORGAN, Telford F., ENS
MORRIS, Albert O., S1 *
MORSE, Kendall H., LT (jg)
MORTON, Charles W., S2
MORTON, Marion E., SK2
MOSELEY, Morgan M., SC1 *
MOULTON, Charles C., S2
MOWREY, Ted E., SK3 *
MOYNELO, Harold C. Jr., ENS
MROSZAK, Francis A., S2
MULDOON, John J., MM1*
MULVEY, William R., BM1*
MURILLO, Sammy, S2
MURPHY, Allen, S2
MURPHY, Paul J., FC3 *

MUSARRA, Joseph, S1
MYERS, Charles Lee Jr., S2
MYERS, Glen A., MM2
MYERS, H. B., F1 *
NABERS, Neal A., S2
NASPINI, Joseph A., F2 *
NEAL, Charles K., S2
NEAL, George M., S2
NEALE, Harlan B., S2
NELSEN, Edward J., GM1*
NELSON, Frank H., S2 *
NEU, Hugh H., S2
NEUBAUER, Richard, S2
NEUMAN, Jerome C., F1
NEVILLE, Bobby G., S2
NEWCOMER, Lewis W., MM3
NEWELL, James T., EM1
NEWHALL, James F., S1 *
NICHOLS, James C., S2 *
NICHOLS, Joseph L., BM2
NICHOLS, Paul V., MM3
NIELSEN, Carl Aage Chor Jr., F1
NIETO, Baltazar P., GM3
NIGHTINGALE, William O., MM1 *
NISKANEN, John H., F2
NIXON, Daniel M., S2 *
NORBERG, James A., CBMP *
NORMAN, Theodore R., GM2
NOWAK, George J., F2
NUGENT, William G., S2
NUNLEY, James P., F1
NUNLEY, Troy A., S2 *
NUTT, Raymond A., S2
NUTTALL, Alexander C., S1 *
OBLEDO, Mike G., S1 *
O'BRIEN, Arthur J., S2
O'CALLAGHAN, Del R., WT2
OCHOA, Ernest, FC3
O'DONNELL, James E., WT3 *
OLDERON, Bernhard G., S1
OLIJAR, John, S1 *
O'NEIL, Eugene E., S1
ORR, Homer L., HA1
ORR, John Irwin Jr., LT
ORSBURN, Frank H., SSML2 *
ORTIZ, Orlando R., Y3
OSBURN, Charles W., S2
OTT, Theodore G., Y1
OUTLAND, Felton J., S1 *
OVERMAN, Thurman D., S2 *
OWEN, Keith N., SC3 *
OWENS, Robert Sheldon Jr., QM3
OWENSBY, Clifford C., F2
PACE, Curtis, S2 *
PACHECO, Jose C., S2 *
PAGITT, Eldon E., F2

PAIT, Robert E., BM2
PALMITER, Adelore A., S2 *
PANE, Francis W., S2
PARHAM, Fred, ST2
PARK, David E., ENS
PAROUBEK, Richard A., Y1 *
PASKET, Lyle M., S2 *
PATTERSON, Alfred T., S2
PATTERSON, Kenneth G., S1
PATZER, Herman L., EM1
PAULK, Luther D., S2 *
PAYNE, Edward G., S2 *
PAYNE, George D., S2
PENA, Santos A., S1 *
PENDER, Welburn M., F2
PEREZ, Basilio, S2 *
PERKINS, Edward C., F2 *
PERRY, Robert J., S2
PESSOLANO, Michael R., LT
PETERS, Earl J., S2
PETERSON, Avery C., S2 *
PETERSON, Darrel E., S1
PETERSON, Frederick A., MAM3
PETERSON, Glenn H., S1
PETERSON, Ralph R., S2
PETRINCIC, John Nicholas Jr., FC3
PEYTON, Robert C., STM1
PHILLIPS, Aulton N. Sr., F2
PHILLIPS, Huie H., S2 *
PIERCE, Clyde A., CWTA
PIERCE, Robert W., S2
PIPERATA, Alfred J., MM1
PITMAN, Robert F., S2
PITTMAN, Almire Jr., ST3
PLEISS, Roger D., F2
PODISH, Paul, S2 *
PODSCHUN, Clifford A., S2 *
POGUE, Herman C., S2 *
POHL, Theodore, F2
POKRYFKA, Donald M., S2
POOR, Gerald M., S2 *
POORE, Albert F., S2
POTRYKUS, Frank P., F2
POTTS, Dale F., S2 *
POWELL, Howard W., F1
POWERS, R. C. Ottis, S2
POYNTER, Raymond L., S2
PRAAY, William T., S2
PRATHER, Clarence J., CMMA
PRATT, George R., F1
PRICE, James D., S1 *
PRIESTLE, Ralph A., S2
PRIOR, Walter M., S2
PUCKETT, William C., S2
PUPUIS, John A., S1
PURCEL, Franklin W., S2

PURSEL, Forest V., WT2
PYRON, Freddie H., S1
QUEALY, William C. Jr., PR2 *
RABB, John R., SC1
RAGSDALE, Jean O., S1
RAHN, Alvin W., SK3
RAINES, Clifford Jr., S2
RAINS, Rufus B., S1
RAMIREZ, Ricardo, S1 *
RAMSEYER, Raymond C., RT3
RANDOLPH, Cleo, STM1
RATHBONE, Wilson, S2 *
RATHMAN, Frank Jr., S1
RAWDON, John H., EM3 *
REALING, Lyle O., FC2
REDMAYNE, Richard B., LT. *
REED, Thomas W., EM3
REEMTS, Alvan T., S1
REESE, Jesse E., S2
REEVES, Chester O. B., S1 *
REEVES, Robert A., F2
REGALADO, Robert H., S1
REHNER, Herbert A., S1 *
REID, Curtis F., S2 *
REID, James E., BM2 *
REID, John, LCDR *
REID, Tommy L., RDM3 *
REILLY, James F., Y1
REINERT, Leroy, F1
REMONDET, Edward J. Jr., S2
REYNOLDS, Alford, GM2 *
REYNOLDS, Andrew E., S1
REYNOLDS, Carleton C., F1
RHEA, Clifford, F2
RHODES, Vernon L., F1
RHOTEN, Roy E., F2
RICE, Albert, STM1
RICH, Garland L., S1
RICHARDSON, John R., S2
RICHARDSON, Joseph G., S2
RIDER, Francis A., RDM3
RILEY, Junior Thomas., BM2
RINEAY, Francis Henry, Jr., S2 *
ROBERTS, Benjamin E., WT1
ROBERTS, Charles, S1
ROBERTS, Norman H., MM1 *
ROBISON, Gerald E., RT3
ROBISON, John D., COX *
ROBISON, Marzie J., S2
ROCHE, Joseph M., LT
ROCKENBACH, Earl A., SC2
ROESBERRY, Jack R., S1
ROGELL, Henry T., F1
ROGERS, Ralph G., RDM3 *
ROGERS, Ross, Jr., ENS *
ROLAND, Jack A., PHM1

ROLLINS, Willard E., RM3
ROMANI, Frank J., HA1
ROOF, Charles W., S2
ROSE, Berson H., GM2
ROSS, Glen E., F2
ROTHMAN, Aaron, RDM3
ROWDEN, Joseph G., F1
ROZZANO, John Jr., S2
RUDOMANSKI, Eugene W., RT2
RUE, William G., MM1
RUSSELL, Robert A., S2
RUSSELL, Virgil M., COX *
RUST, Edwin L., S1
RUTHERFORD, Robert A., RM2
RYDZESKI, Frank W., F1
SAATHOFF, Don W., S2 *
SAENZ, Jose A., SC3
SAIN, Albert F., S1
SALINAS, Alfredo A., S1
SAMANO, Nuraldo, S2
SAMPSON, Joseph R., S2
SAMS, Robert C., STM2
SANCHEZ, Alejandro V., S2
SANCHEZ, Fernando S., SC3 *
SAND, Cyrus H., BM1
SANDERS, Everett R., MOMM1
SASSMAN, Gordon W., COX
SCANLAN, Osceola C., S2 *
SCARBROUGH, Fred R., COX
SCHAAP, Marion J., QM1
SCHAEFER, Harry W., S2
SCHAFFER, Edward J., S1
SCHARTON, Elmer D., S1
SCHECHTERLE, Harold J., RDM3 *
SCHEIB, Albert E., F2
SCHEWE, Alfred P., S1
SCHLATTER, Robert L., AOM3
SCHLOTTER, James R., RDM3
SCHMUECK, John A., CPHMP *
SCHNAPPAUF, Harold J., SK3
SCHOOLEY, Dillard A., COX
SCHUMACHER, Arthur J. Jr., CEMA
SCOGGINS, Millard, SM2
SCOTT, Burl D., STM2
SCOTT, Curtis M., S1
SCOTT, Hilliard, STM1
SEABERT, Clarke W., S2 *
SEBASTIAN, Clifford H., RM2
SEDIVI, Alfred J., PHOM2
SELBACH, Walter H., WT2
SELL, Ernest F., EM2
SELLERS, Leonard E., SF3
SELMAN, Amos, S2
SETCHFIELD, Arthur L., COX *
SEWELL, Loris E., S2
SHAFER, Robert P., GM3 *

SHAND, Kenneth W., WT2
SHARP, William H., S2 *
SHAW, Calvin P., GM2
SHEARER, Harold J., S2 *
SHELTON, William E. Jr., SM2
SHIELDS, Cecil N., SM2
SHIPMAN, Robert L., GM3
SHOWN, Donald H., CFC *
SHOWS, Audie B., COX *
SIKES, Theodore A., ENS
SILCOX, Burnice R., S1
SILVA, Phillip G., S1
SIMCOX, Gordon W., EM3
SIMCOX, John A., F1
SIMPSON, William E., BM2 *
SIMS, Clarence, CK2
SINCLAIR, J. Ray, S2 *
SINGERMAN, David, SM2
SIPES, John L., S1
SITEK, Henry J., S2 *
SITZLAR, William C., F1
SLADEK, Wayne L., BM1 *
SLANKARD, Jack C., S1 *
SMALLEY, Howard E., S1
SMELTZER, Charles H., S2 *
SMERAGLIA, Michael, RM3
SMITH, Carl M., SM2
SMITH, Charles A., S1
SMITH, Cozell Lee Jr., COX *
SMITH, Edwin L., S2
SMITH, Eugene G., BM2
SMITH, Frederick C., F2 *
SMITH, George R., S1
SMITH, Guy N., FC2
SMITH, Henry A., F1
SMITH, Homer L., F2
SMITH, James W., S2 *
SMITH, Kenneth D., S2
SMITH, Olen E., CM3
SNYDER, John N., SF2
SNYDER, Richard R., S1
SOLOMON, William Jr., S2
SORDIA, Ralph, S2
SOSPIZIO, Andre, EM3 *
SPARKS, Charles B., COX
SPEER, Lowell E., RT3
SPENCER, Daniel F., S1 *
SPENCER, James D., LT
SPENCER, Roger, S1 *
SPENCER, Sidney A., WO
SPINDLE, Orval A., S1
SPINELLI, John A., SC2 *
SPOMER, Elmer J., SF2
STADLER, Robert H., WT3
STAMM, Florian M., S2 *
STANFORTH, David E., F2

STANKOWSKI, Archie J., S2
STANTURF, Frederick R., MM2
STEIGERWALD, Fred, GM2
STEPHENS, Richard P., S2 *
STEVENS, George G., WT2 *
STEVENS, Wayne A., MM2
STEWART, Glenn W., CFCP *
STEWART, Thomas A., SK2
STICKLEY, Charles B., GM3
STIER, William G., S1
STIMSON, David, ENS
STONE, Dale E., S2
STONE, Homer B., Y1
STOUT, Kenneth I., LCDR
St. PIERRE, Leslie R., MM2
STRAIN, Joseph M., S2
STREICH, Allen C., RM2
STRICKLAND, George T., S2
STRIETER, Robert C., S2
STRIPE, William S., S2
STROM, Donald A., S2
STROMKO, Joseph A., F2
STRYFFELER, Virgil L., F2
STUECKLE, Robert L., S2
STURTEVANT, Elwyn L., RM2 *
SUDANO, Angelo A., SSML3
SUHR, Jerome R., S2
SULLIVAN, James P., S2
SULLIVAN, William D., PTR2
SUTER, Frank E., S1 *
SWANSON, Robert H., MM2
SWART, Robert L., LT (jg)
SWINDELL, Jerome H., F2
TAGGART, Thomas H., S1
TALLEY, Dewell E., RM2
TAWATER, Charles H., F1 *
TEERLINK, David S., CWO
TELFORD, Arno J., RT3
TERRY, Robert W., S1
THELEN, Richard P., S2 *
THIELSCHER, Robert T., CRTP
THOMAS, Ivan M., S1 *
THOMPSON, David A., EM3 *
THORPE, Everett N., WT3
THURKETTLE, William C., S2 *
TIDWELL, James F., S2
TISTHAMMER, Bernard E., CGMA
TOCE, Nicolo, S2
TODD, Harold O., CM3
TORRETTA, John Mickey, F1 *
TOSH, Bill H., RDM3
TRIEMER, Ernst A., ENS
TROTTER, Arthur C., RM2
TRUDEAU, Edmond A., LT
TRUE, Roger G., S2
TRUITT, Robert E., RM2

TRYON, Frederick B., BUG2
TULL, James A., SI
TURNER, Charles M., S2 *
TURNER, William C., MM2
TURNER, William H. Jr., ACMMA
TWIBLE, Harlan M., ENS *
ULIBARRI, Antonio D., S2
ULLMANN, Paul E., LT (jg)
UMENHOFFER, Lyle E., SI *
UNDERWOOD, Carey L., SI
UNDERWOOD, Ralph E., SI *
VAN METER, Joseph W., WT3 *
WAKEFIELD, James N., SI
WALKER, A.W., STM1
WALKER, Jack E., RM2
WALKER, Verner B., F2 *
WALLACE, Earl J., RDM3
WALLACE, John, RDM3
WALTERS, Donald H., FI
WARREN, William R., RT3
WATERS, Jack L., CYA
WATSON, Winston H., F2
WELLS, Charles O., SI *
WELLS, Gerald Lloyd, EM3
WENNERHOLM, Wayne L., COX
WENZEL, Ray G., RT3
WHALEN, Stuart D., GM2
WHALLON, Louis E. Jr., LT (jg)
WHITE, Earl C., TCI
WHITE, Howard M., CWTP
WHITING, George A., F2 *
WHITMAN, Robert T., LT
WILCOX, Lindsey Z., WT2 *
WILEMAN, Roy W., PHM3
WILLARD, Merriman D., PHM2
WILLIAMS, Billie J., MM2
WILLIAMS, Magellan, STM1
WILLIAMS, Robert L., WO
WILSON, Frank, F2
WILSON, Thomas B., SI
WISNIEWSKI, Stanley, F2 *
WITTMER, Milton R., EM2
WITZIG, Robert M., FC3 *
WOJCIECHOWSKI, Maryian J., GM2
WOLFE, Floyd R., GM3
WOODS, Leonard T., CWO
WOOLSTON, John, ENS *
YEAPLE, Jack T., Y3
ZINK, Charles W., EM2 *
ZOBAL, Francis J., S2

MARINE DETACHMENT

BRINKER, David A., PFC
BROWN, Orlo N., PFC
BUSH, John R., PVT
CROMLING, Charles J. Jr., PLTSGT
DAVIS, William H., PFC
DUPECK, Albert Jr., PFC
GREENWALD, Jacob, 1st SGT *
GRIMM, Loren E., PFC
HANCOCK, Thomas A., PFC
HARRELL, Edgar A., CPL *
HOLLAND, John F. Jr., PFC
HUBBARD, Gordon R., PFC
HUBBARD, Leland R., PFC
HUGHES, Max M., PFC *
JACOB, Melvin C., PFC *
KENWORTHY, Glenn W., CPL
KIRCHNER, John H., PVT
LARSEN, Harlan D., PFC
LEES, Henry W., PFC
MARTTILA, Howard W., PVT
McCOY, Giles G., PFC *
MESSENGER, Leonard J., PFC
MUNSON, Bryan C., PFC
MURPHY, Charles T., PFC
NEAL, William F., PFC
PARKE, Edward L., CAPT
REDD, Robert F., PVT
REINOLD, George H., PFC
RICH, Raymond A., PFC *
RIGGINS, Earl, PVT *
ROSE, Francis E., PFC
SPINO, Frank J., PFC
SPOONER, Miles L., PVT *
STAUFFER, Edward H., 1st LT
STRAUGHN, Howard V. Jr., CPL
THOMSEN, Arthur A., PFC
TRACY, Richard I. Jr., SGT
UFFELMAN, Paul R., PFC *
WYCH, Robert A. PFC

* Indicates a survivor.

Sources:

1. *ONLY 317 SURVIVED!*, authors: USS *Indianapolis* survivors, Copyright © 2002 by USS *Indianapolis* Survivors Organization.

2. *In Harm's Way*, Doug Stanton, (Henry Holt and Company, New York, 2001).

3. Congressional Record, Proceedings and Debates of the 106th Congress, First Session, Vol. 145, No. 76, Washington, D.C.

INDEX

Printed in the United States
36115LVS00007B/52-54